A View from Hereford's Past

A View from Hereford's Past

A report on the archaeological
excavation in Hereford Cathedral Close
in 1993

by
Richard Stone & Nic Appleton-Fox

LOGASTON PRESS

LOGASTON PRESS
Little Logaston Woonton Almeley
Herefordshire HR3 6QH

First Published by Logaston Press 1996
Copyright © City of Hereford Archaeology Committee,
Dean & Chapter, Mappa Mundi Trust and English Heritage 1996

All rights reserved. No part of this publication
may be reproduced, stored in a retrieval system,
or transmitted, in any form or by any means,
electronic, mechanical, photocopying, recording
or otherwise, without the prior permission,
in writing of the publisher.

ISBN 1 873827 39 3

Typeset by Logaston Press
Printed in Great Britain by
Hillman Printers (Frome) Ltd

CONTENTS

	Page
List of Illustrations	vii
Foreword *by The Dean of Hereford*	ix
Preface *by Sir John Cotterell*	xi
Acknowledgements	xii
Introduction	1
The Background: what was known about Hereford before the excavation	3
Saxon Hereford	4
The formal layout of the city	8
The Norman re-organisation	9
The cathedral cemetery	10
The later use of the precinct	12
The Excavation	17
Interim Conclusions from the Excavation	19
The earliest evidence	19
The urban layout	19
The burial ground	22
A cemetery again	24
The plague pits	24
The final stages	25
The population of Hereford and their lifestyle	26
Detailed Description of the Excavation	29
The earliest settlement (Period 1)	29
The late Saxon period (Period 2)	30
The gravel quarry and charnel pit (Period 3)	37
The medieval cemetery (Period 4)	41
The post-medieval use (Period 5)	50
The Finds	55
The Artefacts *by Ros Tyrell*	55
The Coins *by Nic Appleton-Fox*	58
The Human Remains *by Stephanie Pinter-Bellows*	58
The Animal Bone *by Stephanie Pinter-Bellows*	61
The Ceramic Material *by Alan Vince*	62
The Environmental Remains *by Elizabeth Pearson*	64
The Future: what remains to be done *by Ron Shoesmith*	65
Bibliography	67

List of Illustrations

Fig. 1   Location of Hereford
Fig. 2   The vicinity of Hereford in the Roman period
Fig. 3   Taylor's map of Hereford (1757)
Fig. 4   Plan of Hereford, showing principal sites, buildings and roads mentioned in the text
Fig. 5   Outline plan of Hereford in the late Saxon period
Fig. 6   Artist's view of land use around the cathedral in the medieval period
Fig. 7   Enlarged view of the Cathedral Close from Taylor's map (1757)
Fig. 8   Plan of the proposed Music Room (1760), showing the existing boundaries associated with the timber yard
Fig. 9   Print of the collapsed West Front with the Music Room just to the south
Fig. 10   Cathedral Close in 1858 (Curley)
Fig. 11   Artist's impression of the excavation in progress, without its associated paraphenalia
Fig. 12   Detail of the cobbled surface of the late Saxon road (Period 2)
Fig. 13   Possible form of the house above the late Saxon basement
Fig. 14   The charnel in the pit (Period 3)
Fig. 15   Skeletons in the southernmost mass grave of the medieval cemetery, presumably a plague pit
Fig. 16   Plan of the excavation, Period 1
Fig. 17   Skeleton 3843, with the arms in the pelvic area and a barrel padlock by the left side of the pelvis
Fig. 18   Plan of the excavation, Period 2
Fig. 19   Foundation trench 4107
Fig. 20   The stone-lined basement 4254
Fig. 21   Skeletons of two dogs in the late Saxon cesspit
Fig. 22   Plan of the excavation, Period 3
Fig. 23   Skeleton 4116, with pillow stones
Fig. 24   Skeleton 4145, lying prone
Fig. 25   Skeleton 3851, with separated skull 3850
Fig. 26   Slumping of the backfill of the charnel pit from the south, with the period 5 foundation trench 0048 cut through it
Fig. 27   The two campaigns of levelling up as a result of the slumping of the pit
Fig. 28   Plan of the excavation, Period 4, showing some of the earlier graves
Fig. 29   Grave 3008 containing skeleton 3007 with stone lining, after removal of the stone capping
Fig. 30   Skeleton 3616, with a spread of mortar, perhaps a foundation for a monument, to the west
Fig. 31   Plan of the excavation, Period 4, showing the mass graves
Fig. 32   Flexed skeleton (1691) in the central mass grave
Fig. 33   Plan of the excavation, Period 4, showing some of the later burials and the avoidance of the area of the mass graves

Fig. 34 Detail of foetus 3410 and the mother 3409
Fig. 35 Skeleton 2883, the arms folded across the stomach
Fig. 36 Skeleton 0959, the arms folded on the chest
Fig. 37 Plan of the excavation, Period 5
Fig. 38 Pit 0079
Fig. 39 Barrel padlock, Period 2
Fig. 40 Shroud buckle, with leather, Period 4
Fig. 41 Sword, Period 2
Fig. 42 Book clasp
Fig. 43 Bone object, possibly a handle
Fig. 44 Apple corers, Period 5

Foreword

None of us knew when the building of the new library was begun in January 1993 just how fascinating an archaeological project it would prove to be. The Dean and Chapter and the Mappa Mundi Trustees were determined, with the help they had received from John Paul Getty and from the National Heritage Memorial Fund, to build a fitting home for both the Mappa Mundi and the historic Chained Library. It was an exciting project, not only because it would reunite both halves of the Chained Library and show them together for the first time since the 1840s, but also because of the opportunities it would give for an interpretative exhibition which would explain both the Mappa Mundi and the Chained Library to visitors.

All this has meant considerable movement in the life of the cathedral and the change of use of several parts of the building. Certain of these changes have already happened. In order to free the South Cloister as a home for the interpretative exhibition, the Song School has been moved to a new site in College Cloisters and the modern theological library which the cathedral maintains has been moved to the top floor of the new library, and is already open to the public. The Cathedral Restaurant is in the process of being moved from the Bishop's Cloister, and these various moves have enabled us to take down the partitions and see the cloisters in all their beauty for the first time for well over a century.

The eleventh century wall of the old two storey chapel which used to stand in the bishop's garden has also been revealed by the removal of the bookcases. By the time Her Majesty the Queen opens the new library in May, the crypt of the cathedral will also have been reopened as a quiet space with the removal of the Mappa Mundi to its new home, and the relocation of the Treasury.

All this has involved archaeology, but the digging of the basement of the new library proved unexpectedly to be a very exciting project indeed, the results of which are still being assessed. It is very good to see the beginnings of this assessment taking place and we are all very grateful to Ron Shoesmith, Richard Stone, Carolyn Heighway and all who have helped them in this dig, which has proved of such interest. The findings of the archaeology which has been so much a part of this whole project are not only fascinating for us as a cathedral foundation, but also have given insights into the life of our city in earlier days. This book begins to draw together some of these findings and it is a very welcome addition to our developing knowledge of both city and cathedral.

Robert Willis
Dean of Hereford

Preface

Bishop John Easthaugh asked me in 1989 to work with him to form a Trust, whose prime responsibility was the maintenance and display of the Mappa Mundi, Chained Library and the ancient manuscripts then in the ownership of the Dean and Chapter of Hereford Cathedral. The National Heritage Memorial Fund gave an endowment of £2m and Mr. Paul Getty gave £1m to meet the cost of housing the Mappa Mundi and Chained Library, which would then be owned by the Trust.

From the beginning the Trustees were determined to maintain the historic link between the Cathedral and its possessions. They, therefore, determined to site the building as near to the Cathedral as possible. We were aware that the whole of the Cathedral Close was an archaeological site of national importance and we realised that any development would mean that we would have to undertake an archaeological excavation. We invited the City of Hereford Archaeology Unit to carry out the initial investigations and to try to give us some idea of the cost. It was agreed between the Trust and the Unit that the south-west corner of the Close would best meet the requirements of the Trust and would be likely to be the least significant in archaeological terms. Various estimates were made as to the likely number of skeletons that would be found. The general consensus seemed to lie between 200 and 400. There were some higher estimates but none of them were anywhere near the final figure of over 1,100. This much higher number had very serious financial implications and meant that the whole of our budget for archaeology was used up on the excavation, leaving us with no funds to meet our obligations for the post-excavation work. We are aware of our responsibilities to complete this work and are seeking more funding to achieve this.

My Trustees and I would like to place on record our gratitude for the skill and expertise shown by the Hereford City Archaeology Unit under its Director, Mr. Ron Shoesmith, and, in particular, the Project Director, Mr. Richard Stone, and all who took part in the project. The supervision of the whole scheme was carried out conscientiously by the then Cathedral Archaeologist, Ms. Carolyn Heighway.

Sir John Cotterell

Acknowledgements

On any archaeological project of this size a vast number of people are involved. The authors would like to thank first of all the Mappa Mundi Trust, who funded the excavation, and Dean and Chapter who controlled the administration. English Heritage funded the latter part of the excavation and the post-excavation work so far undertaken, as well as giving much valuable advice throughout the project, Brian Kerr being instrumental in this. The project was helped by the co-operation of the architects, Whitfield Partners, the Cathedrals Fabric Commission and Hereford City Council. The archaeological consultants to the project, Carolyn Heighway and Martin Biddle, ensured that the project proceeded smoothly and efficiently. Thanks are also due to the authors' then employer, the City of Hereford Archaeology Committee, particularly the chairman, the late Dick Vowles, and to the permanent staff of the City of Hereford Archaeology Unit, its operating arm, for administrative as well as practical assistance.

The consultant specialists Alan Vince, Clare de Rouffignac, Liz Pearson, Juliet Rogers, Brian Gilmour and Jacqui Watson have all been instrumental in the understanding of various aspects of the archaeological record. The consultant osteologist Stephanie Pinter-Bellows, must be singled out for particular thanks, for the expertise she brought to all aspects of the on and off site work associated with the vast amounts of human bone.

Special thanks are due to the whole of the excavation staff. Ros Tyrrell (Finds Supervisor) worked wonders to ensure that all the material was processed and properly stored, including tons of human bone, as well as contributing to this volume. Alex Thorne and later George Children (Planning Supervisors) coped superbly with all the planning and on site drawing, and also produced some of the illustrations. The rest of the team coped superbly with the large numbers of skeletons and other remains, both in the excavation and processing of finds and bone: Katie Anderson, Chrissie Atherton, Jill Bailey, Mike Bardill, Dan Barrett, Jeannie Bradley, Paul Cox, Alison Denton, Gary Edmonson, Chrissie Freeth, Catriona Gibson, Peter Hart, Russell Heath, Tim Hoverd, Isca Howell, Lucy Howell, Will Johnston, Steve Macklin, Jim Marsh, Jonathan Mullis, Dave Murray, Louise Muston, Loretta Nikolic, Trish O'Connell, Jonathan Roberts, Dale Rouse, Ewen Rutter, Huw Sherlock, Ian Smith, Paul White. Without their unfailing efforts the project could not have been a success. Thanks also to the many volunteers (56 in total) who assisted during and after the excavation, particularly to Tess Ormerod and Megan Brickley.

The authors are grateful to the Dean of Hereford and to Sir John Cotterell for their contributions to this volume and to the project as a whole. In the stages leading to publication helpful advice and comments were given by Ron Shoesmith and Richard Morriss of the City of Hereford Archaeology Unit, Kate Clark of English Heritage and Andy Johnson of Logaston Press. Any inaccuracies or omissions of course remain the responsibility of the authors.

Richard Stone and Nic Appleton-Fox
February, 1996

Introduction

The archaeological excavation in the south-west corner of the Cathedral Close came about when it was agreed to re-house various treasures belonging to the cathedral—including the thirteenth century Mappa Mundi, the Chained Library, and an extension to the Archives—in a new building to be erected next to the Dean Leigh Library. This building, two storeys above ground with a basement below, would necessarily destroy all the archaeological remains in the area and the project was mounted to excavate, record and interpret the finds.

Evidence of continuous occupation dating from the Saxon period was found. Part of the cemetery associated with the Saxon cathedral was excavated, together with a late Saxon building containing a basement, which fronted on to a road leading north from the river Wye. A vast pit, filled with the bones of some 5,000 people and dating to the early twelfth century, was then dug through the earlier levels. Later in the medieval period the area again became a cemetery, and over 1,000 burials were excavated, nearly 200 of which came from three mass graves which are likely to date from the time of the Black Death in the mid fourteenth century.

The excavation has produced a vast amount of information, especially about the life and death of the inhabitants of Hereford. The full analysis of this information has yet to be undertaken, but when it has it should result in a much greater depth of understanding. In this research it will be important not only to interpret the archaeology in terms of Hereford, but also to place it within a wider context, comparing Hereford with other towns and cities throughout the country.

Clearly, the major thrust of the research work will be concerned with the human remains, a large collection of which have been retained for further examination. This is one of the largest assemblages to be excavated in the country. It is of especial interest as it can be sub-divided into smaller groups by period, but also by considering the mass burials separately it will provide a 'snap-shot' of a cross-section of the population. The results of this analysis will be compared with analyses of other human remains excavated in the city and with large skeletal assemblages of similar date found elsewhere in the country, such as those from Barton-on-Humber and St Gregory's Priory in Canterbury.

The topography of the city and aspects of town planning in the Saxon period are also major research topics. The stone basement, so far unique, is of particular interest, especially as it is associated with a lost road layout which may date to the earliest years of the settlement.

A wealth of information on the environment and the exploitation of local resources, as well as of trade, has been gathered. Analysis will be designed to answer specific questions about the development of the city and thus provide a better understanding of several aspects which have been addressed by previous writers.

The background—what was known about Hereford prior to the excavation

Hereford lies on the north bank of the river Wye, a few miles to the east of the border between England and Wales (Fig. 1). Several factors associated with the geology of the area and the river itself have made this a particularly desirable location for a settlement. Above the Old Red Sandstone, which forms the main geological stratum in this part of the county, is a thick deposit of gravel left by the Wye glacier during the final glaciation. The immediate city area consists of a shallow south-facing gravel terrace, sloping down towards the river, with some terracing in the last 100 metres. It is well enough drained to give good building conditions, and several springs and streams leading to the river from the north have ensured an ample supply of fresh water.

The area on the southern bank of the river is liable to flood, but this is only a slight problem on the northern bank. During summer the river is shallow and the sites of two fords have been suggested, one to the south of Broad Street, the other to the east of the castle.

There is only very slight evidence of any occupation during the prehistoric and Roman periods in what is now Hereford. Hill forts of Iron Age date are liberally scattered around Herefordshire with the major fort at Credenhill some seven kilometres to the north-west. There are several Roman settlements in the neighbourhood including the town of *Magnis* (Kenchester) and Roman roads are known within a short distance of the city (Fig. 2).

It is possible that there may have been a small settlement in or near Hereford during the Roman period, for the main Roman road from Chester to Caerleon may, at one time, have crossed the river Wye at one of the Hereford fords. Nevertheless, the known course of the road follows what appears on the map to be a diversion to *Magnis*, seven kilometres to the west-north-west, where a bridge was probably built across the Wye. There could have been another, more direct road passing through Hereford, perhaps with Kenchester effectively on a side road, but so far no archaeological evidence to confirm this hypothesis has been found. Another factor is the east-west road—called the Roman Road—which forms the northern boundary of the city. Perhaps a road branched off this to lead through Hereford, crossing the Lugg at Mordiford, and continuing south-eastwards to the important Roman town of *Glevum* (Gloucester).

However, direct evidence for a Roman settlement in the immediate vicinity of Hereford is very sparse. The possibility of a Roman fort has been considered and even its presumed size and location calculated (Marshall, 1940, 68-70), but no hard evidence has been found to substantiate the hypothesis. Three altars and a bronze statuette have been recovered in the city, but these could well have been brought from elsewhere at a later date. Similarly, there have been several finds of coins, sherds of pottery and fragments of tile, but none of these have been in features which can be shown to be of Roman date and are presumably pieces of rubbish deposited at later dates. Certainly there have been no structural remains from this period. All the available archaeological evidence points to the origin of the settlement being at a later date, probably well into the Saxon period.

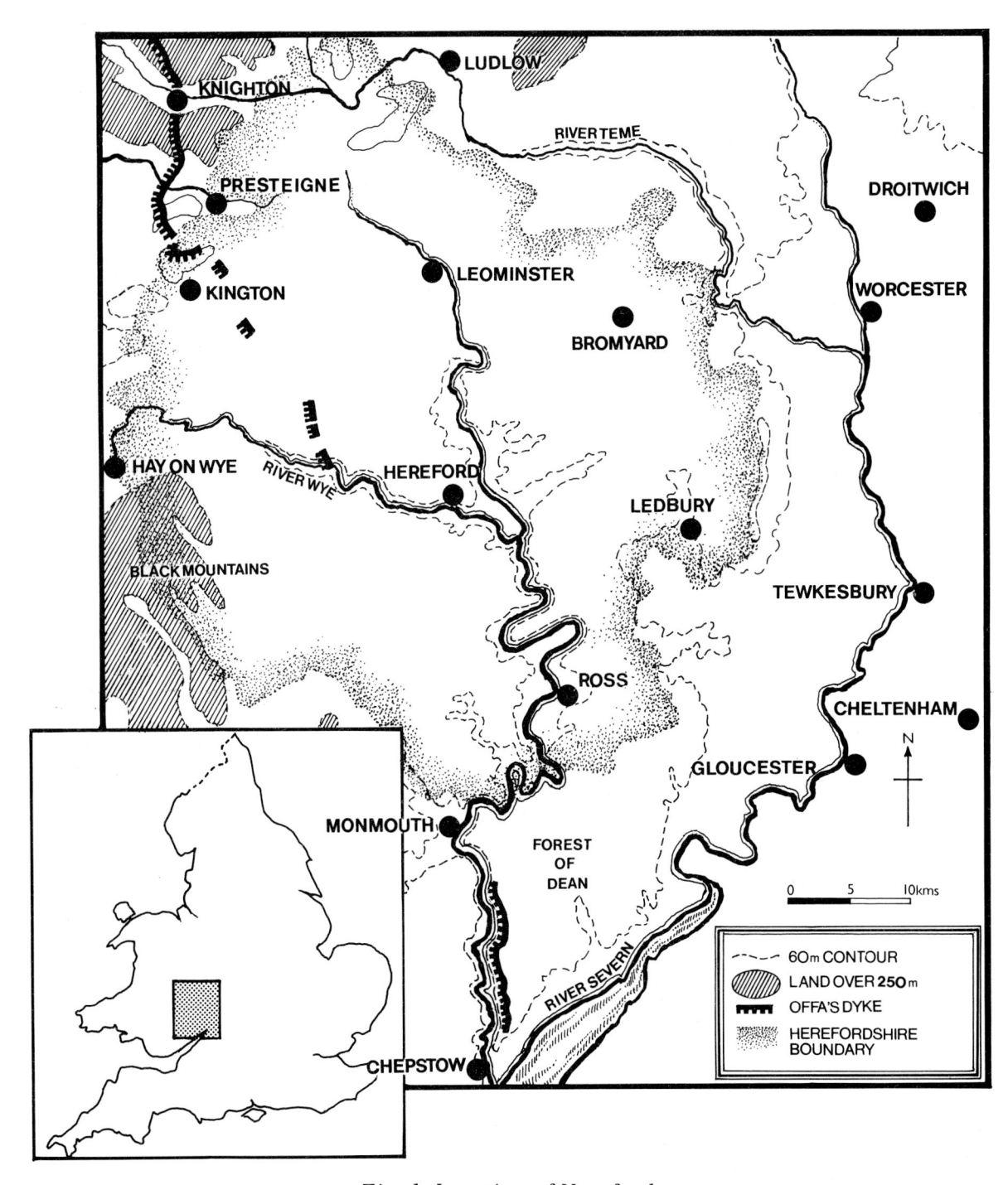

Fig. 1. Location of Hereford

Saxon Hereford

The foundation of a monastic community, later dedicated to St Guthlac, in what is now Castle Green, has been suggested to date from around 540 AD (Whitehead, 1980, 4). The community probably had access to a ford across the Wye at the southern end of the appropriately named Britons Street (now Mill Street) and excavations on Castle Green in 1960 and 1973 showed that the religious settlement, including burials, was probably established before the eighth century (Shoesmith, 1980, 90). More recently, however, it has been convincingly argued that St Guthlac's was not such an early foundation and that the cathedral was the oldest religious settlement (Barrow, 1992, 81). This is based on parish boundaries which emphasise the central position, and thus the early origin, of the cathedral. (Figs. 3 & 4)

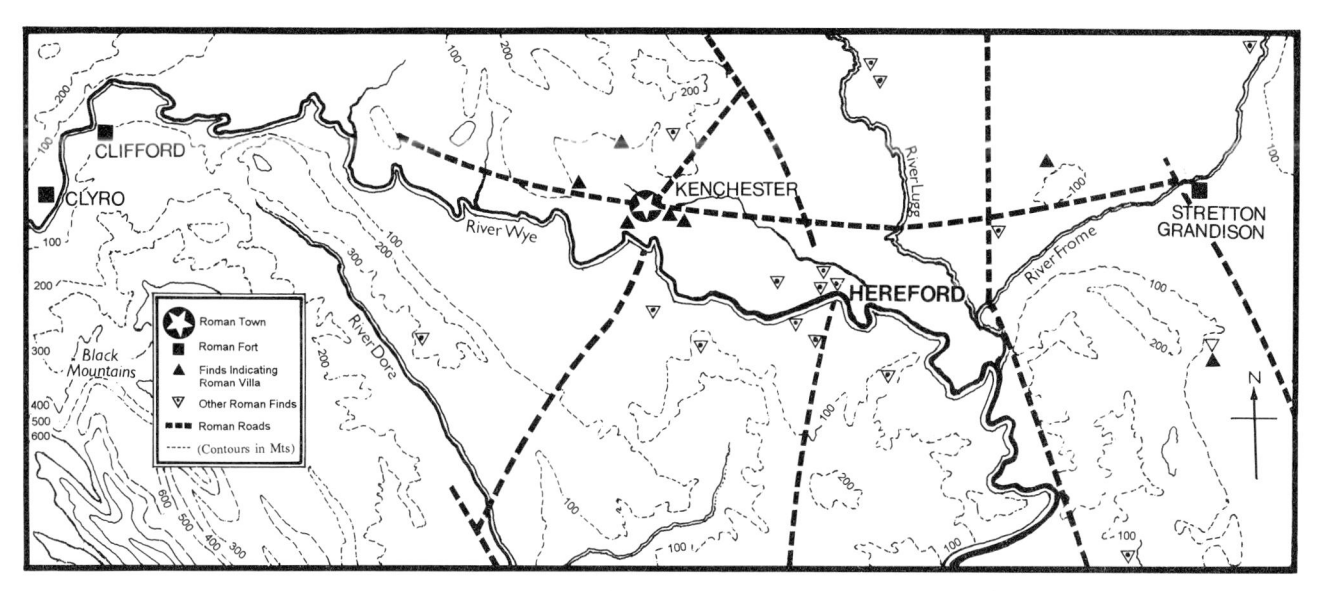

Fig. 2. The vicinity of Hereford in the Roman period

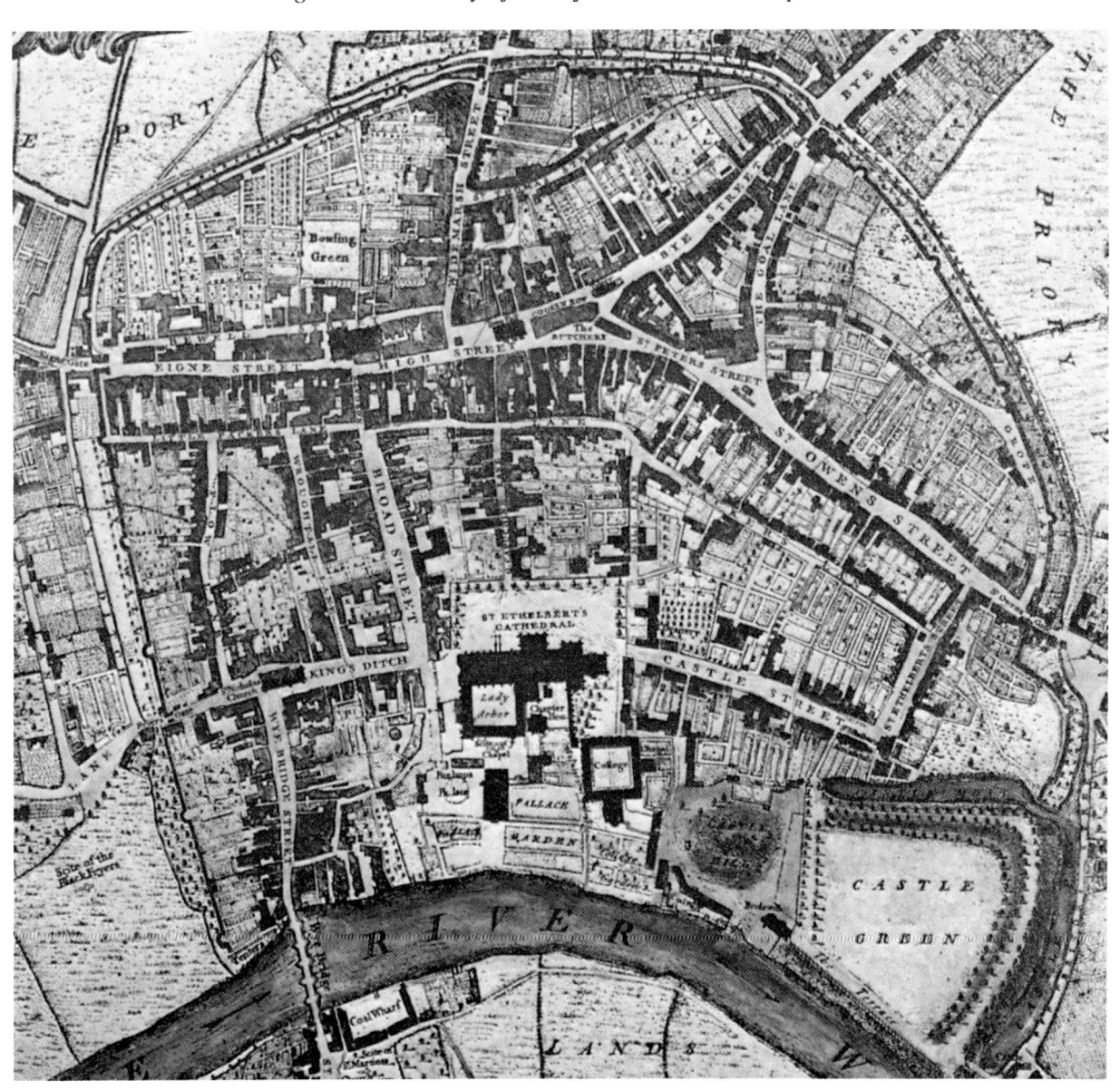

Fig. 3. Taylor's map of Hereford (1757)

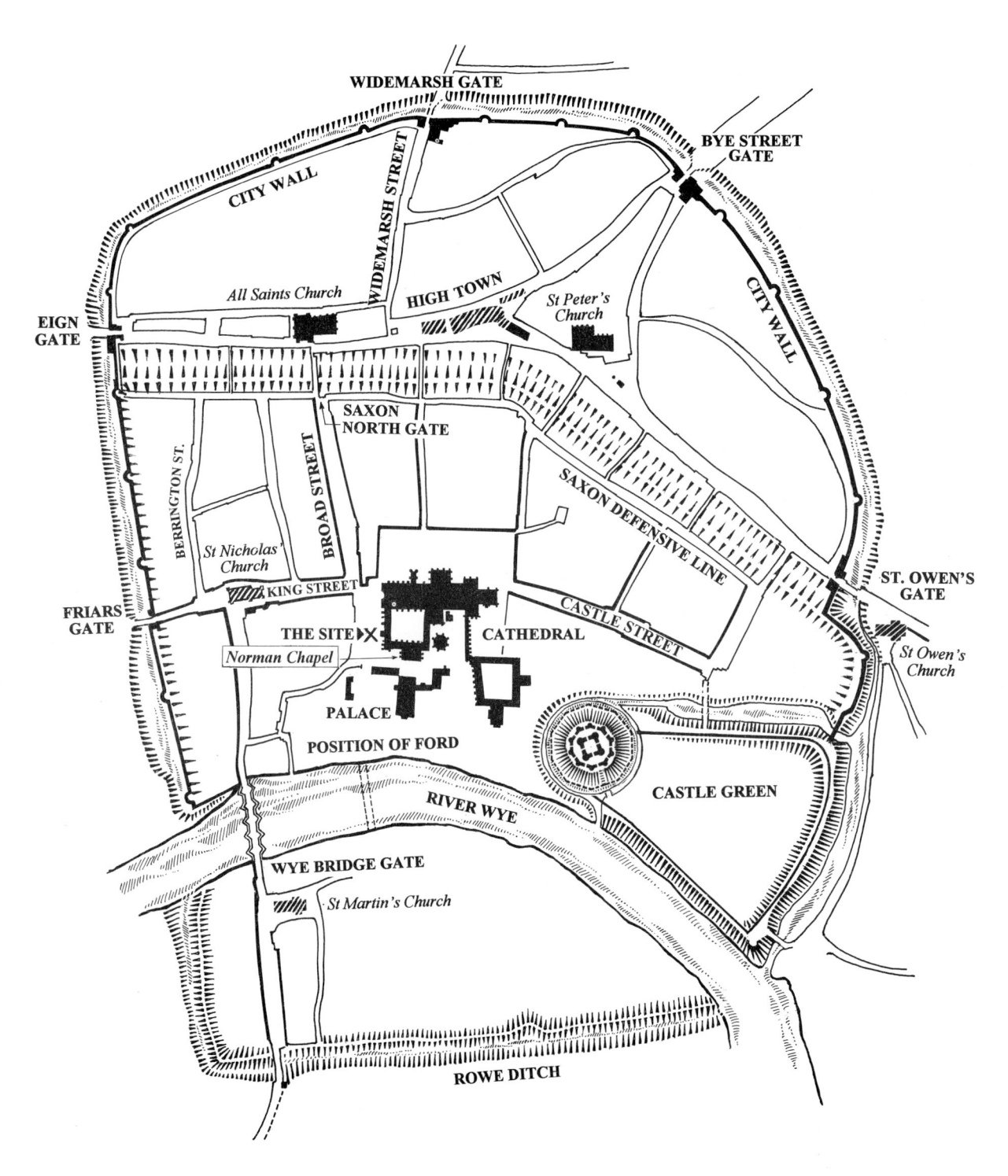

Fig. 4. Plan of Hereford, showing principal sites, buildings and roads mentioned in the text

A foundation date in or before the late seventh century for the cathedral can be suggested from the appointment in 676 AD of a certain Putta as bishop of a new diocese in this region. However, there is some dispute as to whether this diocese was actually centred on Hereford. Lydbury North, Ledbury and Leominster all have claims to be the then seat of the bishopric, but recent research suggests it was indeed at Hereford (Barrow, 1993, xxvii). It is known from a twelfth century document that a cross was erected by Bishop Cuthbert (736-740) commemorating the building of a new burial place for three earlier bishops (Hamilton, 1870, 163).

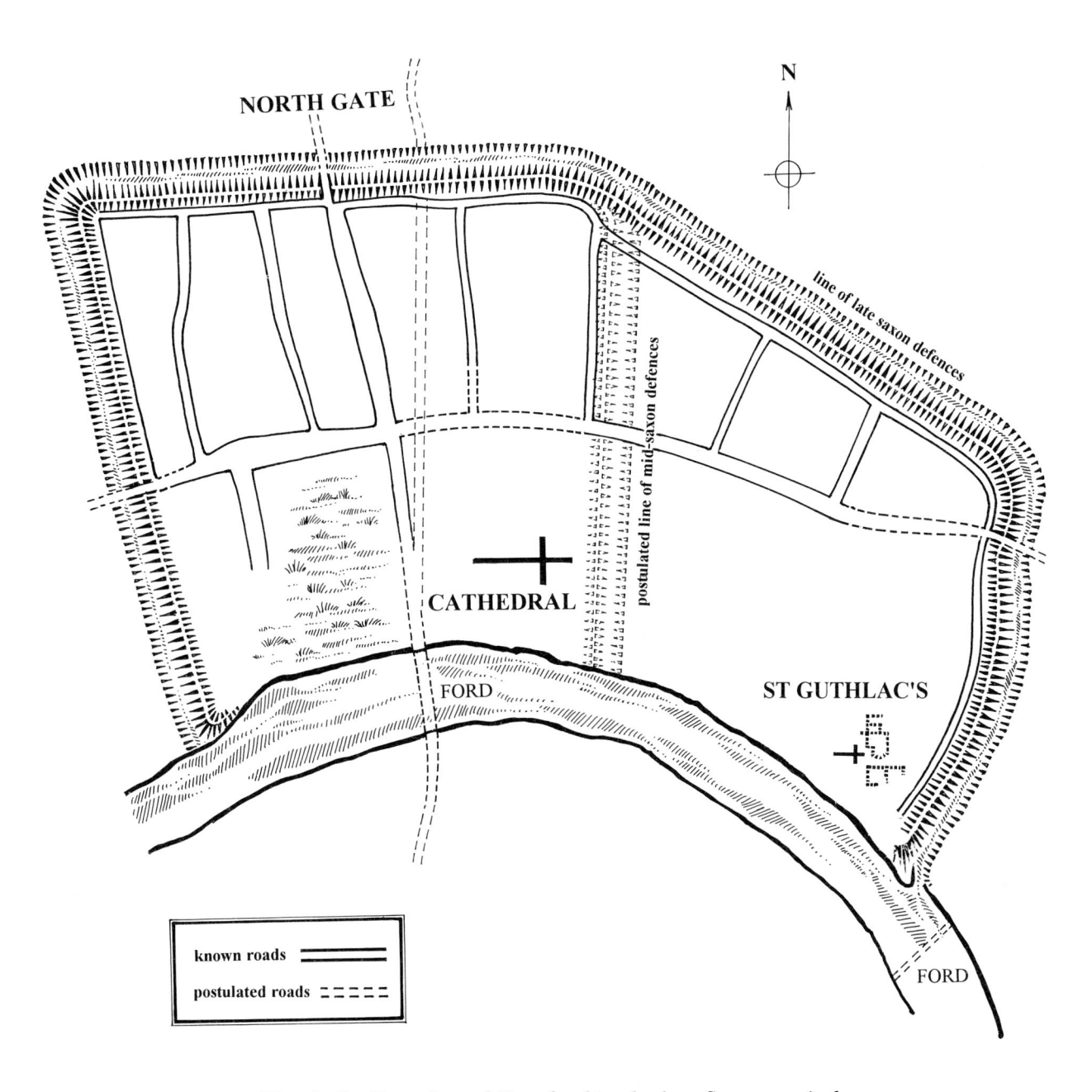

Fig. 5. Outline plan of Hereford in the late Saxon period

Unfortunately, it is not clear whether this translation was from one town to another, from one part of a town to another, or simply from one part of a church or graveyard to another (Whitehead, 1980, 3).

The first documentary reference to anyone specifically calling himself bishop of Hereford was Wulfheard around 803-805 (*Cart. Sax.* 315). By this time the see was clearly based in Hereford and there would therefore have been a cathedral church.

Elsewhere in the city, excavations have demonstrated that settlement was well established, having begun perhaps as early as the middle of the seventh century, with an established sequence of buildings at sites between Victoria Street and Berrington Street by the early ninth century (Shoesmith, 1982, 72-3).

At this time the settlement extended more than 500 metres from east to west and, in some parts at least, as far as 300 metres from north to south (Fig. 5). This early growth probably began as a response to the topographic importance of the area as a river crossing, with the ford south of Broad Street as the major focus in the later Saxon period. The first occupation to develop alongside the ford could well have been secular rather than ecclesiastical. Whichever came first, the central focus of the settlement was near the cathedral and would have been occupied earlier than the outer areas such as St Guthlac's monastery and the area around Victoria Street.

The road layout at this period would have related to the cathedral and the ford. In the early twentieth century the possibility of a road leading north from the ford to join the present day Widemarsh Street was suggested (Watkins, 1920, plate facing 249). The main east-west road may also have been in place by the early eighth century, situated about 150 metres north of the river and more or less running parallel with it. (Shoesmith, 1982, 91 and fig 141).

The formal layout of the city
By the end of the ninth century, when Alfred was on the throne, the situation had radically altered and Hereford had become a fully fledged city. The cathedral was at its centre and a planned layout, incorporating formal defences and a grid of roads, had been established (Shoesmith, 1982, 74).

The earliest defence, perhaps dating to the middle of the ninth century, may have been based on boundary ditches of late eighth century date in some areas. This defence, which consisted of a gravel rampart and probably an external ditch, has only been found at the west of the city. The extent of the original defended area is therefore uncertain, but it is suggested that St Guthlac's monastery lay to the east, beyond the defensive line.

In the late ninth or early tenth century the defences were extended and reinforced, providing the town with a wide, deep ditch in front of a timber-faced embankment. The northern defences ran parallel to the Wye, with the east and west arms running at right angles down to the river. This enlarged defended circuit included the monastery of St Guthlac and, by the mid-tenth century, was strengthened by the addition of a stone wall.

Much of the Saxon road grid survives to the present day. It was based on a road leading north from the river, incorporating Broad Street, and an east-west road. The two ends of this road survive as Castle Street to the east, and King Street and St Nicholas' Street to the west, although the central part is now lost. The junction of these two major thoroughfares formed a central cross-roads, and subsidiary north-south streets were laid to either side, with an intra-mural road inside at least the northern part of the defences.

In 1980 a deep trench dug for laying telephone cables along King Street revealed a continuous line of timbers laid above a water-logged area. These presumably formed part of a roadway which crossed the marshy area known as Kings Ditch. The date of the timbers has been established with 95% certainty by carbon dating to between 900 and 1200 AD, so the roadway may be a late Saxon consolidation of the main thoroughfare across the city.

The Saxon cathedral must have been somewhere in the area to the south-east of the cross-roads. Its position is uncertain, but about 1650 Silas Taylor found 'beyond the lines of the present building, and particularly towards the east, near the cloisters of the college, such stupendous foundations, such capitals and pedestals, such well-wrought bases for arches, and such rare engravings, and mouldings of friezes' as left little doubt in his mind that they were the foundations of the Saxon cathedral (Duncumb, 1804, 523). As the cathedral was a minster church and the centre of the diocese a large part of its precinct would have included the cemetery, though the existence of another late Saxon cemetery associated with the monastery of St Guthlac's demonstrates that the cathedral did not then have a monopoly on burial rights as it did later in the medieval period. The entire precinct or Close associated with the cathedral would have been to the south of the main east-west road, perhaps extending south as far as the river. It could have included the area now occupied by the twelfth century Bishop's Palace grounds and may well have been bounded on the west by the road leading north from the ford. The staff of the cathedral are likely to have been lodged within the precinct and, although the site of the original residence of the bishop is unknown it could well have been close to its present location.

The market place, a major focus of the city, probably extended along the centre of Broad Street and adjacent streets although there may have been a formal, centralised, market, perhaps to one side of the central cross-roads along one of the main roads. Whichever was the case, this would have been an important commercial area and would have had relatively substantial buildings. After the Norman Conquest the Saxon market place became redundant, and later changes have obscured the form of this part of the early city.

From the middle of the tenth century there seems to have been a period of peace and stability in the surrounding area and the defences were allowed to fall into disrepair. In the middle of the eleventh century the cathedral was rebuilt by bishop Athelstan (1042-1056). Was this the building whose remains were seen by Silas Taylor to the south-east of the present cathedral? The peaceful climate was gradually changing and, despite the building of a castle around 1052 by the new Norman earl, Ralph, the city was sacked by the Welsh in 1055 (Shoesmith, 1982, 94). The extent of damage to Athelstan's cathedral is debatable as, when the bishop died in 1056, he was buried 'in the church which he had built from the foundation.' (Whitehead, 1980, 15) The re-fortification of the defences by Earl (later King) Harold in 1056 was clearly a response to this attack.

The Norman re-organisation

The earliest period for which contemporary documents relating to Hereford survive in any quantity is after the Norman Conquest. Similarly, there are no standing buildings earlier than this date in the city. The later eleventh century was a time of major change, politically, culturally, and economically. Norman influence in the city had begun slightly earlier than the Conquest, with a Norman earl from around 1046, and a Norman bishop, Walter, from 1060. In 1067, almost immediately after the Conquest, the Earldom of Hereford passed to William FitzOsbern. He was responsible for laying out a new market place and settlement for Norman immigrants to the north of the Saxon defences. The old Saxon market would then have gradually fallen into disuse.

The Conquest also had a dramatic effect on the layout of the cathedral precinct. The first major change came between 1079 and 1095 when Bishop Robert Losinga built a two-storey chapel to the south of the present cloister. Its northern wall was later incorporated into the fifteenth century south range of the cloister and this is the only part of the chapel to have survived the demolition in 1737. When this double chapel was built, Athelstan's cathedral was presumably still the main focus of the precinct.

Soon after this, during the episcopate of Bishop Reynhelm (1107 to 1115), a start was made on the construction of a new cathedral. It was laid out to the north of the presumed site of the Saxon cathedral and cut across the line of the main east-west road through the city.

The building of the new cathedral would have been a vast undertaking and, in the nineteenth century, when some of the foundations of the nave were exposed they were seen to be in trenches about 3.5 metres wide, and were laid on the natural gravels which were 2.1 metres deep (Willis, 1841, 7). This cathedral emphasised the pre-eminence of the new Norman regime both in political and spiritual matters. It took several decades to complete and required a high level of organisation and a large labour force. Much of this Norman work survives in the present building, though there have been many alterations and restorations during the ensuing centuries.

In addition to this new church other buildings, including residences for the Dean, canons and other clerics employed by the cathedral, continued to be constructed around the edges of the precinct throughout the medieval period. One of the most important of these was the Bishop's Palace. Towards the close of the twelfth century a new hall for this was built to the south of the new cathedral and Losinga's two-storey chapel. This was a substantial aisled hall built of massive timbers and much of it survives encased in the post-medieval palace (Blair, 1987).

By the end of the twelfth century the layout of the whole of the ecclesiastical area had been greatly altered from its late Saxon form. The precinct extended further north to its present boundary, incorporating properties that had been on the north side of the Saxon east-west road and effectively closing this road. To the south, the precinct may have become smaller, with the whole area from the Losinga Chapel southwards to the river being given over to the bishop.

Interestingly, the three major ecclesiastical Norman buildings—the cathedral, the Losinga Chapel and the Bishop's Palace—all have slightly different orientations. This is significant as they may be survivals of earlier alignments which are otherwise lost. Perhaps the Losinga Chapel was aligned with the Saxon cathedral, whilst the Bishop's Hall may reflect the line of the edge of the river terrace or of the road leading northwards from the ford.

Although the cathedral was not monastic and was served by secular canons, it was usual for all cathedrals to be provided with a cloister that included a chapter house. Hereford was no exception, with cloistral ranges to the south of the cathedral and north of the Losigna Chapel.

The cathedral cemetery

In the Saxon period both St Guthlac's and the cathedral had burial rights. However, it is known from documentary evidence that by 1108 at the latest the cathedral was claiming exclusive burial rights within the city (Barrow, 1992, 81). After the monastery of St Guthlac had been moved to a new site outside the city walls in 1143, its old graveyard was undoubtedly closed for general burial. The only burials excavated from this cemetery which could be later than this date were infants (Shoesmith, 1980, 30). By this time the burial rights of the cathedral had effectively been secured over all the parishes of the city and its suburbs, as well as over several of the outlying parishes. This was important as the fees that were payable for each burial generated much revenue for the cathedral. A large area was needed for the graveyard and, by the later medieval period, burial rights probably extended throughout the whole open area of the present Close.

The earliest direct reference to a cathedral cemetery is in 1140, although the earlier existence of one is clear (Barrow, 1992, 81). The presence of a cemetery in the middle of the city, where there was increasing pressure on space, inevitably led to some degree of misuse. The first documented example of such profanation was a mandate of 1180-86 from Bishop Robert Folliot ordering the Dean and Chapter to remove a house that had been built in the cemetery and which used to belong to the archdeacon. At the end of the fourteenth century Richard II became involved in the problem, granting a licence to enclose the cathedral cemetery in order to stop the:

> many dangers and moral scandals...viz., thefts of church goods, the secret burial at night of unbaptized infants and again the bodies of the dead there have been grubbed up by swine and other animals, and frequently there have been occasions of immorality and other misprisons and contentions to the great peril of souls and grave scandal of the said church and its ministers (Capes, 1908, 84).

The graveyard was clearly not the quiet, well-tended resting place that would be expected today and, despite Richard II's efforts, the abuse continued (Fig. 6). On one occasion in 1434 this was particularly acute and Bishop Spofford addressed all these problems, requiring the Dean and Chapter 'within twenty days to remove all trading and servile work, and stop all animals from entering the cemetery, enclosing it with lock and key' (Morgan, 1976, 15). However, as

Fig. 6. Artist's view of land use around the cathedral in the medieval period

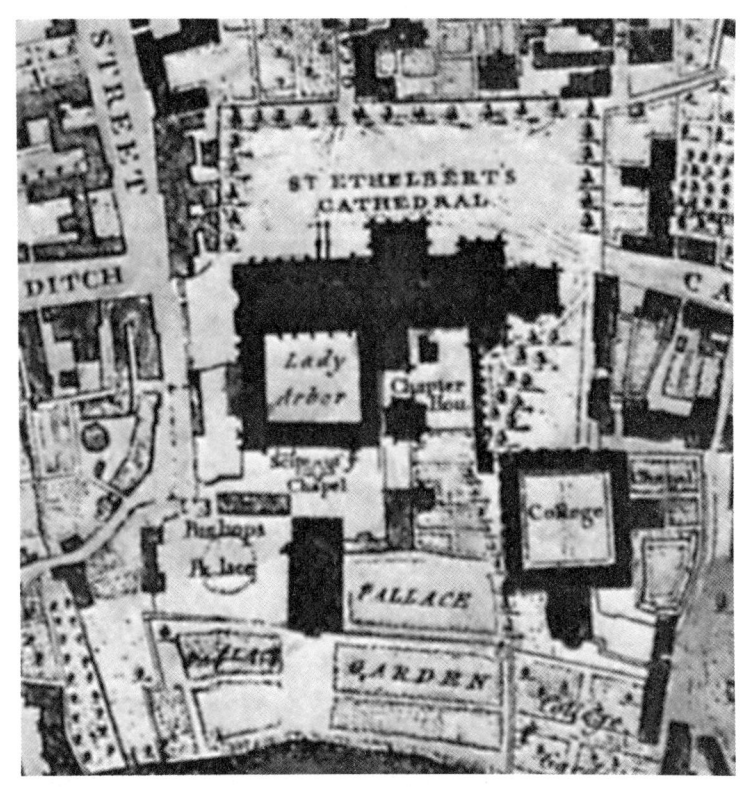

Fig. 7. Enlarged view of the Cathedral Close from Taylor's map (1757)

several bishops' registers continue to note these problems, the Dean and Chapter clearly needed reminding of their duties every so often.

There were other pressures on the precinct as well as the cemetery, including buildings that were needed for the cathedral community. The elaborate fourteenth century chapter house, finally demolished in 1769 after damage sustained during the Civil War, was one of these, and its presence strongly suggests that the present, fifteenth century, cloister was a replacement for an earlier one.

At some time in the post-medieval period the area just to the west of the western arm of the cloister, which had previously been part of the cemetery, was given over for use as a garden. In 1741 this land was transferred from the common fund to the fabric fund and later references refer to 'the former garden' (Hughes, 1994, 2). The transfer from one cathedral account to another probably reflects this change of use. From this time until 1760 the area was in use as a timber yard serving the cathedral. The boundary of this yard and the buildings on the site are apparent on Taylor's map of 1757 (Fig. 7).

Elsewhere in the precinct the cemetery continued in use, and the eighteenth century proved to be a time of good management. There are many references to tree planting and felling, and the upkeep and alteration of paths through the cemetery.

Despite this good management, the cemetery eventually became overcrowded and in 1791 the precinct was closed as a general burial ground. This was to avoid any 'contagious Distemper' and because of 'how highly indecent it is and improper to observe the many putrid limbs continually thrown out' (Morgan, 1976, 17). These and other such contemporary comments indicate that the monopoly on burial rights which the cathedral had previously enjoyed had eventually become a problem and action had to be taken both for the health of the citizens and for the sake of propriety. From this time on burial was increasingly the responsibility of the individual parishes using new or much enlarged parish graveyards. This problem of overcrowding was by no means confined to Hereford, and an Act of Parliament was passed in 1853 to stop general burial in urban areas.

The later use of the precinct
In 1760 the west range of the cloister was totally demolished and the timber yard was moved into the Chapter House garden. This fifteenth century range had for a while been used by the Free Grammar School but had long been in a state of disrepair. The opportunity to upgrade the site was taken in a very forward looking way. It was to continue to be used by the school, but was also to become one of the venues for the Three Choirs Festival. Rather than replacing the

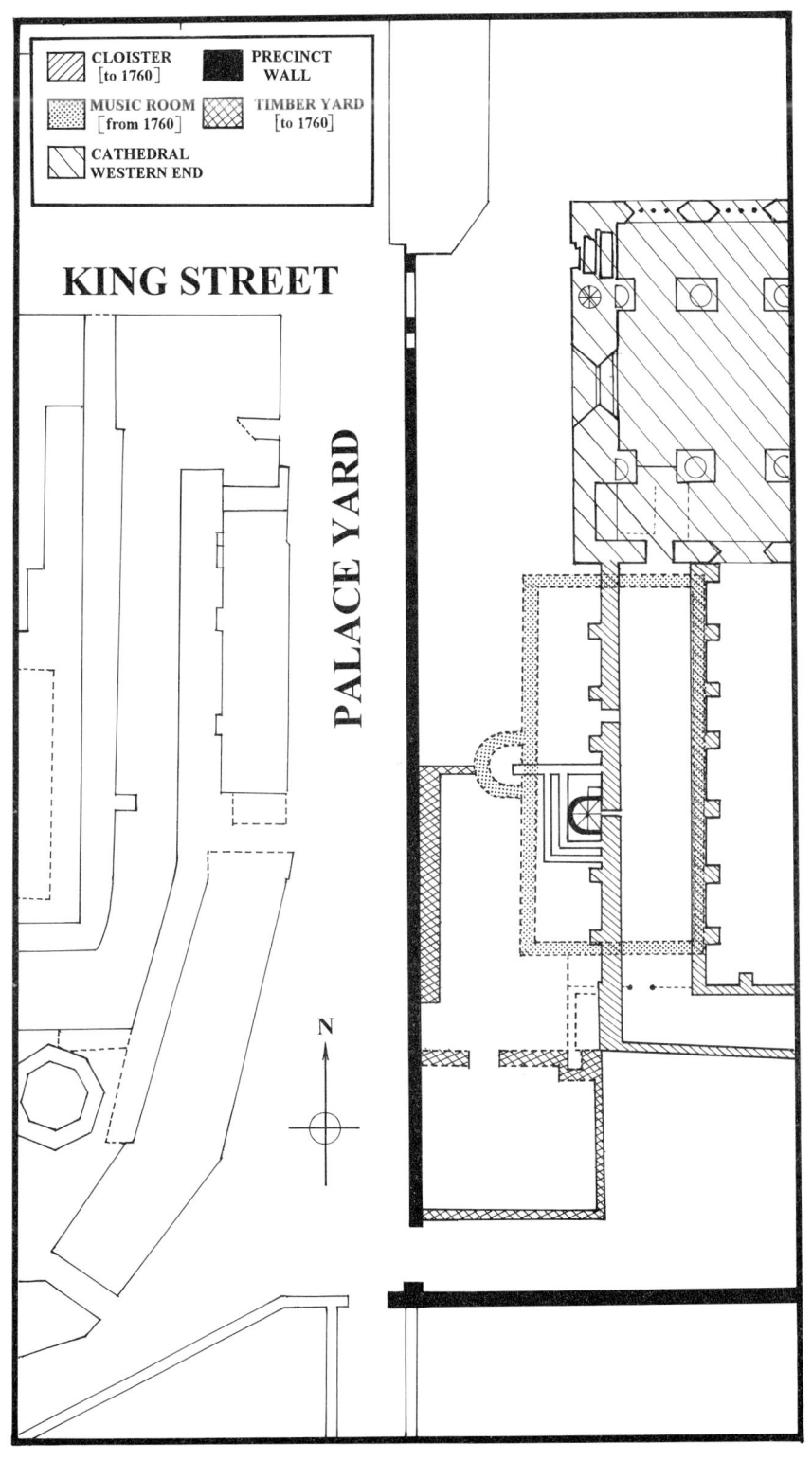

Fig. 8. Plan of the proposed Music Room (1760), showing existing boundaries associated with the timber yard

old building with a standard claustral range, the new building, called the Music Room, was a substantial brick structure, much wider and far more spacious than its predecessor (Fig. 8).

It was built in the new Georgian style and opened in 1762, with the piece of ground in front laid open 'in order to form a more Commodious way to the said New Edifice'.

A few years later, on Easter Monday 1786, a catastrophe occurred. The Norman west front of the cathedral fell, due to structural failure. Incredibly, this collapse only slightly damaged the Music Room directly to the south (Fig. 9). Despite this remarkable survival and modifications carried out in the early nineteenth century, the Music Room was demolished in 1835, a victim of changing architectural taste. The southern part of the space left after its demolition was filled in 1897 by the construction of the Dean Leigh Library. In the meantime the west front of the cathedral had been rebuilt rather blandly by James Wyatt around 1793, and was then totally redesigned in 1904.

It was only in 1845 that the precinct was first referred to as Cathedral Close. Shortly after, there was a major landscaping of the Close designed to present a open lawn traversed with paths (Fig. 10). This work, undertaken in 1850-1, involved the lowering of the ground level in parts of the Close by several feet. This means that many of the burials that had originally been deeply interred are now just below

Fig. 9. Print of the collapsed West Front with the Music Room just to the south

the surface. Indeed, one observer recalled that 'the Churchyard ... had been recently lowered, and I was told that the earth, including fragments of coffins and bones which were discreetly overlooked, had been carted away and deposited in a pit somewhere in the Barton' (Humfrys, 1925, 1). Since then, Cathedral Close has remained largely unchanged, the skeletons buried just beneath our feet.

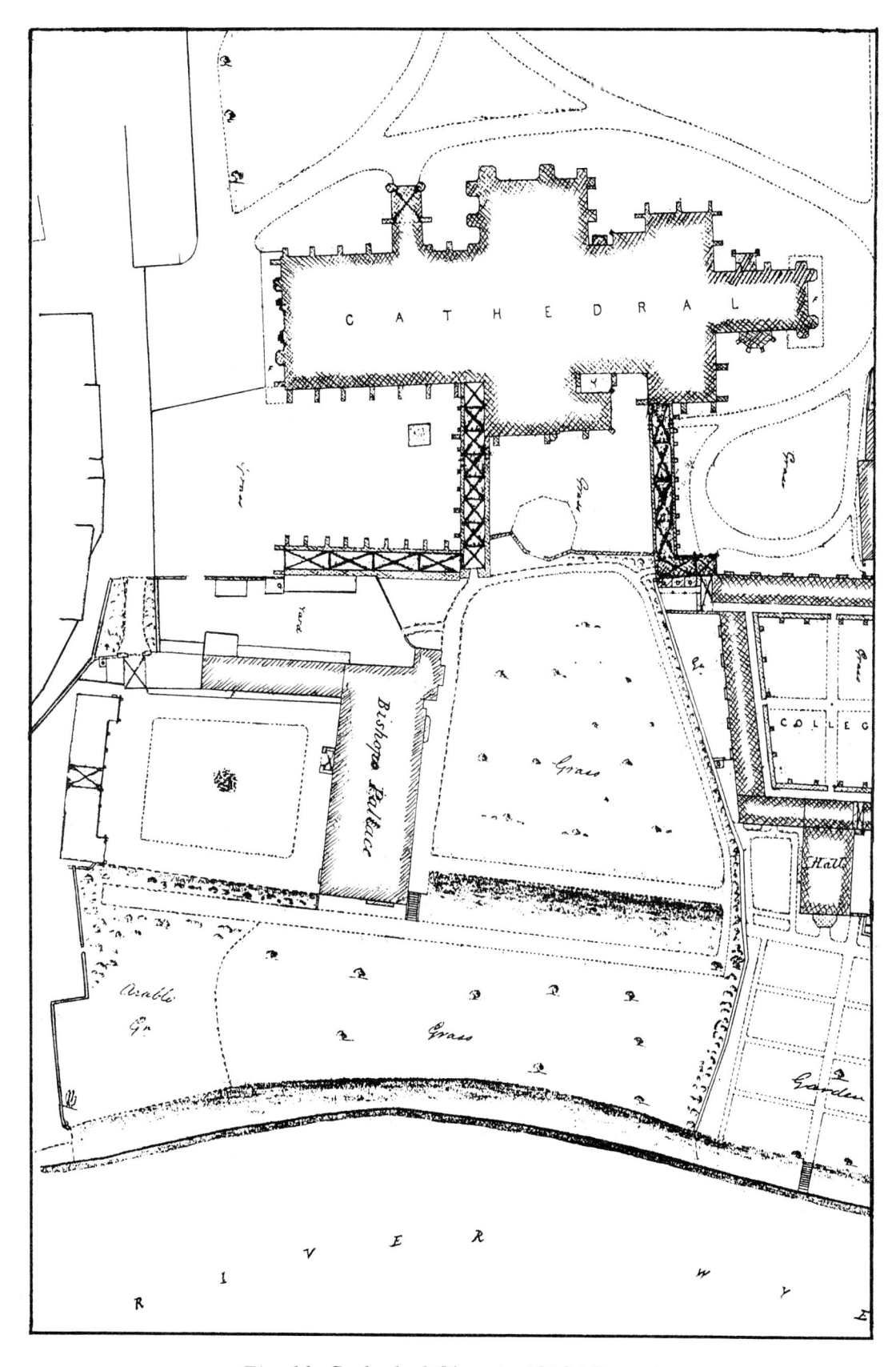

Fig. 10. Cathedral Close in 1858 (Curley)

The Excavation

The eventual decision to erect the new building in which to display the Mappa Mundi and Chained Library in this area was taken after much consideration of various possible locations. It was finally decided that the position to the west of the cloister, adjoining the Dean Leigh Library, was most desirable as it was sufficiently close to the cathedral, whilst also being acceptable to the Local Authority in terms of townscape. At the time the area had three uses: the southern half was hard standing, with a path leading north along the west side of the Dean Leigh Library; the north-west part was lawned and had a hawthorn tree at the centre; whilst the north-eastern corner included a temporary mason's yard.

It was appreciated well in advance of the construction of the new building that the site had considerable archaeological potential. Initially a desk-based survey of the area was commissioned from the City of Hereford Archaeology Unit. This report, produced early in 1991, summarised the history and known archaeology of the site and concluded that it was of national importance, with buried deposits lying close to the surface. It was considered that excavation could unearth evidence relating to the medieval cemetery, to the Anglo-Saxon street pattern, and to the early cathedral(s). Later features that could be encountered included a putative twelfth century precinct boundary wall, together with remains of the west claustral range that had been demolished in 1760. There could also be some remains of the West Front which fell in 1786, and evidence of the landscaping of the Close in the nineteenth century.

Evaluation excavations on the site were not considered practicable and in July 1991 a borehole survey was commissioned by the architects in order to investigate engineering and archaeological matters. The City of Hereford Archaeology Unit examined the cores but stressed that archaeological interpretation from such boreholes could only be provisional. However, the cores indicated that there were archaeological deposits up to one metre thick below the cemetery deposits, themselves up to 0.6 metres thick. These layers were covered by a similar thickness of further occupation material. The water table was substantially lower than the deepest occupation levels, so water-logging was not expected.

In order to obtain more detailed information a geophysical survey was commissioned by the architects and carried out by Stratascan. The work entailed the use of resistivity, magnetometry and ground-probing radar, both within the confines of the site and extending beyond it to the north and west. Features identified within the footprint of the proposed building included a pit with rubble tip lines, possible graves and metal coffin fittings, and the line of the footings of the demolished Music Room. In the area to the north (not subsequently excavated) there was evidence for a buttressed wall, two possible foundations or tombs and another large pit. It was concluded that apart from 'isolated blocks of masonry or foundations there appear to be no substantial structures' in the area due to be excavated, and that the survey had 'confirmed ... the evidence for the demolition of the known buildings in the area'.

The Dean and Chapter's archaeological consultant produced a brief for the proposed excavation and a project proposal produced by the City of Hereford Archaeology Unit was accepted.

It was envisaged in the brief that the excavation would find up to 400 burials with some underlying occupation levels and that the average depth of the excavation would be no more than 2 metres. On this basis it was calculated that the excavation operating with a team of sixteen site workers would last between four and six months starting in January 1993. In order to minimise the loss of time due to adverse weather conditions, a temporary cover of clear corrugated plastic on a frame of scaffolding was erected over the whole site.

As the excavation proceeded the inaccuracy of the predictions gradually became apparent. The two most serious variations were, firstly, a pit not found by the radar survey that was some 5.5 metres deep and covered a third of the excavated area, and secondly a total of 1,129 burials over the whole site. As the problems became apparent, it was agreed that the time for the excavation should be extended, ultimately to 34 weeks, and that more staff would be recruited, with up to 25 being employed at any one time. Additionally, volunteers were encouraged. The continuation of the excavation through the summer months created almost Middle Eastern conditions as the cover remained in place. Despite regular watering by hose the ground became very dry and, during the hot sunny days of 1993, it became akin to working in a greenhouse.

Fig. 11. Artist's impression of the excavation in progress, without its associated paraphenalia, the cobbled road on the left, the late Saxon basement centre top and the gravel pit, later used to rebury disarticulated bone from the cathedral cemetery

Interim Conclusions from the Excavation

The detailed description of the excavation which follows this summary has been split into five chronological periods. The first runs from the earliest occupation on the site to late Saxon times. Ditches, pits and post holes indicated some use of the site during either the Roman or, more likely, the early to mid Saxon period, but there was no clear evidence of the nature of that use. The second period extends through the late Saxon period to around 1100. During this time the eastern part of the site became a cemetery and a cobbled road was made along the west of the site, with a building with a basement erected between the road and the cemetery. The third period is quite short. It involved the digging of a vast pit, probably for gravel associated with the building of the Norman cathedral at the start of the twelfth century. The pit was quickly filled, largely with the bones of at least five thousand people, presumably those originally buried where the cathedral now stands and disturbed during the construction works. The fourth period, was the re-establishment and use of the cemetery, continued until the sixteenth century. A total of 1,085 burials were excavated from this cemetery, 189 of them being from three mass graves of late fourteenth or early fifteenth century date and probably victims of the plague. The final period covers the site after use as a cemetery ceased. After being a garden and then a timber yard, the Music Room was built in 1760 on part of the site, the rest again becoming a garden. The Music Room was demolished in the 1830s and the area has since remained open.

The earliest evidence
Little information has been added to what is known about the earliest inhabitants of Hereford. In the area excavated the natural gravels were overlain by a silty soil, representing the original turf line. Several shallow pits and stakeholes give an indication of early occupation, but did not contain any datable material. The only substantial feature which could be of Roman date is a ditch that ran north-south through the western part of the site. It may be possible to obtain a radio-carbon date from the animal bone from this ditch. If the bones are of a mid or late Saxon date then the Roman 'rubbish' must have been deposited later. If the bones date to the Roman period then there is a much greater probability that the ditch is Roman. However, the animal bones could also have been a later deposit, brought in with the Roman waste tile.

Whatever the case, enough of the early levels survived to establish that there was no intensive Roman occupation in this area of Hereford. This strengthens the argument that there was no settlement of any size in this central part of Hereford during the Roman period, and certainly no fort.

The urban layout
The north-south cobbled road with building plots fronting onto it is of critical importance in understanding the original layout of the city. It was clearly in use over a relatively long period as it was re-surfaced several times. The addition of a drain at the side of the road indicates both concern with sanitation and the road's importance. The absence of any ceramic material in Hereford before the middle of the tenth century has meant that the date at which this road was

first laid out is not clear. Before that date, instead of pottery wooden, leather and metal vessels were used. Metal would usually be melted down for reuse when the object became unserviceable, and wood and leather do not tend to survive in Hereford because of the nature of the soils and the ground conditions.

The road, which presumably continued south to the ford, was certainly in use by the eleventh century, but may pre-date the layout of the regular road system in the city which is dated to the late ninth or early tenth century. The road is slightly to the east of the present east side of Broad Street and was on a slightly different alignment. The Bishop's Palace, built some 35 metres to the east of the road line, shares its alignment. As the palace is of late twelfth century date, by which time the road was no longer in use, the alignment may perpetuate some earlier, now lost, feature also associated with this road system. Alternatively, as the road is not on the same alignment as the eleventh century Losinga Chapel, it may imply

Fig. 12. Detail of the cobbled surface of the late Saxon road

that its alignment was of no importance when buildings were laid out within the cathedral precinct. However, the conundrum may be answered by the Saxon cathedral which was still standing when the chapel was built and the new building could well have been aligned with its larger neighbour.

The course of the road northwards from the excavated area is uncertain, but Isaac Taylor's 1757 map of Hereford appears to provide some evidence to substantiate Alfred Watkins' claim that originally the road from the ford may have joined up with Widemarsh Street. On Taylor's map, the common rear boundary of the properties at the north-west corner of Cathedral Close (demolished in 1934) is not, as one would expect, parallel to Broad Street, but diverges from it on the same angle as the road uncovered during the excavation. Its continuation would then have formed a straight line midway between Church Street (Capuchine Lane on Taylor's map) and Broad Street (Watkins, 1920, plate facing 249).

Further to the north, close to the present East Street (Packers Lane on Taylor's map), the rear boundary between properties in Broad Street and those in Church Street also coincides with the line of the road. To the north of East Street this postulated road would have continued northwards to join up with Widemarsh Street. The buildings between East Street and High Town are a later medieval infilling on the old Saxon defensive line. If this interpretation is correct then this road would have had to be earlier than the defences and the establishment of the planned ninth century street system. The basic grid of this element of town planning—reflected in Berrington, Aubrey, Broad and Church streets—is on a different alignment to the excavated road.

It is equally possible that the line of the excavated road changed direction slightly at the crossing with the east-west road and then followed the line of Broad Street to the north. This would mean that the dog-leg at the northern end of Broad Street, in the area shown as Norgate on Taylor's map, is of early origin. The name Norgate and the narrow section of Broad Street are both further indications of the likely northern entrance to the late Saxon town.

A third possibility is that the crossing of the two roads may have been staggered, as was the case at the burh of Cricklade in Wiltshire, whose layout is considered to be slightly later than that of Hereford.

The urban character of the road, suggested by the metalling and particularly by the drain, is reinforced by the presence of the building with the stone basement. Although its date of construction is uncertain it was in use at the latest by the late eleventh century. This building and other stone foundations further to the south were aligned along the road and although it is uncertain whether the latter was part of a building or merely a boundary wall, it is clearly another indication of the urban character of the area as a whole.

This layout may be of help in determining the extent of the jurisdiction of the cathedral authorities. In the same way that the major east-west street (joining King Street to Castle Street) is likely to have formed the northern boundary of the precinct, the north-south road from the ford may well have been the western limit. It is, therefore, likely that the land to the east of the road, together with houses on that land, was owned by the Church.

The use of stone for the buildings implies a relatively high status for this locality. The use of face and core technique as seen in the basement is a constructional method that was known to the Saxons before any Norman influence, though it is more commonly associated with Norman culture. The Norman influence of Earl Ralph from the 1050s and Bishop Walter by the 1060s would also allow for a construction date in the Saxon era.

The reason behind constructing a building with a basement in this late Saxon period is uncertain. No similar building of this date has previously been recognised in Britain, so the cultural implications are poorly understood. Nothing was found during the excavation to suggest the original use of the basement, apart from the implications for the status of the owner. If this area was indeed within the cathedral precinct, as seems likely, the basement may have formed a part of the lodgings (common or otherwise), of the cathedral staff, perhaps even of the bishop.

As the building fronted onto a major road it is possible that it was rented out by the cathedral authorities. The basement could have been used as a secure area, perhaps for one of Hereford's seven Saxon moneyers (Morris, 1983). Equally, the basement may have been a warehouse, perhaps with a shop above and a hall and living accommodation to the south.

A thick layer of refuse that accumulated in the basement indicates a major change in use of the building, and perhaps a change of status of the area as a whole. This could reflect the change of political supremacy, after the Normans had gained control in Hereford. In this case the use of the area as a latrine or cesspit may have been more than a pragmatic use of a redundant building. To complicate matters, a Saxon pattern-welded sword was found at the bottom of this accumulation of refuse. Could it have been left, or hidden and subsequently forgotten, or just dropped?

Fig. 13. Possible form of the house above the late Saxon basement

The burial ground

The western edge of the Saxon cemetery was found just to the east of the stone basement. The density of burial in the small area examined and the presence of at least three generations of graves indicate that use of this area as a graveyard was of long standing. It is likely that there was already some pressure on space, as cemeteries are normally less densely packed towards the periphery.

A large pit dug through the site to a depth of more than five metres, cut through the existing cemetery and the edge of the road. At the same time the south wall of the basement was entirely removed, so either the associated building had fallen into disuse or it was demolished as part of the digging of the pit. It is clear that there must have been a total change in the land use over a wide area, with this part apparently becoming a gravel quarry to provide material for the foundations of the new cathedral.

All but 23 of the individuals represented by the enormous quantity of human bone which had been dumped in the charnel pit in the early twelfth century had originally been buried elsewhere and were interred in the pit as disarticulated bones. The vast amounts of bone were layered with soil. For the most part, these would have been people who died before the Norman Conquest, although their reburial took place shortly after that event.

It has been estimated that the bones represent at least 5,000 people, indicating very large scale graveyard excavations in the vicinity. One possible cause of such an excavation is during the Anarchy, when the castle was garrisoned for King Stephen, whilst Geoffrey Talbot fortified the cathedral tower and surrounding ground. This is based on a reference in 1138 when Robert de Bec describes the digging of a trench, in an unspecified location, which disturbed many burials. Another possibility, equally remote, is that the bones may have been dug up as new buildings were erected in the part of the castle that contained the cemetery associated with St Guthlac's monastery. In either case it is unlikely that such a large number of burials would have been disturbed. Additionally, they would have required transportation for some distance to this site—and do not provide any reason for the initial digging of the pit.

Fig. 14. The charnel in the pit

The most likely interpretation is that the excavations were associated with the building of the Norman cathedral. This was begun during the episcopacy of Bishop Reynhelm (1107-15) and would have had a major impact on Hereford, both politically and due to the disruption to the normal routine. A large number of people would have been employed in the initial site preparation and subsequent construction, together with others further afield in the quarries and those responsible for transportation. The whole area would have become a large building site with redundant buildings, or those simply in the way, being demolished and all traces of earlier graveyards could have been completely lost.

Meanwhile, the trenches for the foundations and the stripping of the ground to allow floors to be laid would have disturbed any burials on the actual site of the new building. The area chosen for the new cathedral must have been adjacent to the existing Saxon cathedral and thus in a place where there were likely to have been earlier burials. It is, therefore, surely from this building work that this vast amount of human bone came—bone that was rapidly re-buried in the deep hole left by the digging of a pit for gravel to be used in the construction of the cathedral. The wholesale disruption of the area probably led to the disuse of the early road along the west of the excavated area and its move further westwards to the line of the present Palace Yard.

Even with this large scale work, the number of disturbed burials could be considered excessive. It may be that some of the bone from the pit emanated from a charnel house—a store for bones exhumed when new graves were dug. If there had been a charnel house on the site of the new cathedral, this would explain why so many bones had to be buried.

Nevertheless, 5,000 burials is a huge number, particularly as the Domesday Survey mentions that in 'Hereford before 1066 there were only 103 men dwelling inside and outside the wall'. In addition to these 'men' there would have been women, servants and children, but this is unlikely to bring the total population even as high as 1,000. The 5,000 or so recovered from the pit could therefore represent the entire population of Hereford for some five generations—about 150 years. As it has been suggested that the cemetery at St Guthlac's on Castle Green could account for a population of up to 800 for 500 years, the sheer quantity of bones in this pit create a problem.

However, there are two factors which may indicate that the burial ground could have filled up more quickly than suggested above. Firstly, the creation of a new market place in 1067 and the tax advantages offered to Norman settlers in the city suggests a rapid growth in population following the Norman Conquest—so more people would have been buried towards the end of the eleventh century. Secondly, and perhaps more importantly, by the end of the twelfth century or earlier the cathedral had burial rights over several parishes outside the city. As minster churches, both St Guthlac's and the cathedral would also have had jurisdiction over several smaller churches over a wide area and this larger population may have been buried in their cemeteries.

Although almost all of the bone from the pit was disarticulated twenty-three complete and partial skeletons were also found. Some of these may have been laid to rest elsewhere, and reburied before they had decayed, but others were certainly buried in this pit as their intended resting place, laid on top of human bone and with a covering of further bone. The pit was not just a convenient hole in which to rebury the bone, it was also a cemetery in its own right.

To twentieth century views this treatment of the dead may seem inappropriate, but cemetery clearances were necessary, and they still happen today. There would almost certainly have been a Christian service to cover such a major reburial, though there would have been an element of mistrust because of the belief in the physical resurrection of the body on Judgment Day. If the body was mixed up with some 5,000 others how could it be resurrected? Were the population's fears allayed because the whole scheme was within the cathedral's control, or did the Church go ahead despite wide misgivings in order to complete the new glorious place of worship?

A cemetery again
After the initial filling of the gravel pit with bone and soil, and after substantial settlement had taken place and the ground had twice been re-levelled, the whole of the site was once again used as a cemetery. This use began probably in the latter part of the twelfth century and continued to some time in the sixteenth, when this part of the cemetery was closed. During this period some 1,100 individuals were buried.

Over time there were changes in burial practices. The standard manner of laying out the corpse—supine with legs extended, in an individual grave—did not alter, but the later interments more commonly had the arms either over the chest or across the stomach, as opposed to the prevailing position in the earlier burials where the arms were in the pelvic area or laid by the sides. The few stone-lined graves from the earliest part of this phase represent a form of burial not apparent in the Saxon period, and are of twelfth or thirteenth century date.

The plague pits
The discovery of three mass graves laid out in a row, of broadly similar dimensions, strongly suggests a major disaster. Nearly two hundred individuals were excavated from these pits and there had clearly been more buried in them, some having been disturbed by post-medieval excavations, indicating that some 300 or 400 were originally interred. Indeed, it is quite possible that further pits exist in the Close to the north of the excavated area.

Fig. 15. Skeletons in the southernmost mass grave of the medieval cemetery, presumably a plague pit

The Black Death is seen as the most probable cause and it appears from the way that the bodies were deposited in the pit that several were brought on carts and put in the pit at one time. This was borne out by thin layers of clay covering several bodies at a time. This would have given some protection against the stench of decaying bodies and was probably an attempt to ward off infection.

Despite what must have been a very high mortality rate, there was still a formality about the burials, with most of the interments in the mass graves being buried according to normal practice. Those few that were buried east-west could easily have been accidentally put in the wrong way around for they would have been buried wrapped in sheets that covered the whole body and knotted at top and bottom. However, those that were laid north-south or south-north, at the eastern edge of the grave, or followed the irregular southern edge of the southern mass grave, bear witness to the need to fill up the graves with as many bodies as possible. As there was no further mass grave to the south, though there was space for one, it is highly likely that this was either the first or last such grave in the row to be dug.

The final stages
The excavation of a large pit through one of these mass graves, in the middle of the sixteenth century, was probably for gravel extraction. It suggests that by this time the area was seen as being outside the cemetery and that any association with an epidemic had probably been forgotten. Thereafter, pits were periodically dug along this western side of the excavation and this, coupled with the general lack of sixteenth century and later finds from grave fills, indicates that perhaps by 1550 the whole of the area had ceased to be used as a cemetery. There is docu-

mentary evidence referring to the use of this area as a garden by 1741, but such a use may have commenced much earlier.

Little can be said about the site after it ceased to be used as part of the cemetery. The removal of several feet of soil during the 1850/1 landscaping of the Close took with it any evidence for the change of the use from cemetery to garden to timber yard, for the ground surfaces relating to these later uses were totally lost. Only deep features survived, such as some of the pits along the western edge of the area excavated. All that remained of the 1760 Music Room were the foundations. There were no traces found of the cathedral's collapsed Norman West Front. After the landscaping the area became an open, grassed area extending east into the cloister. In 1897 the Dean Leigh Library was built, restoring the line of the southern part of the fifteenth century cloister. The new library building now joins the western side of this building.

The population of Hereford and their lifestyle
The study of such a large number of burials of late Saxon and medieval date will eventually allow a good picture to be built up of the physical make-up of previous generations of Herefordians. The site need not be viewed in isolation, for there will be the opportunity to correlate the information with that from the excavation at the Saxon cemetery at Castle Green and with monastic burials at St Guthlac's as well as with other sites throughout the country.

The city's location near the English-Welsh border would have led to intermarriage between the Saxons (the local Magonsaete), their British predecessors, the Welsh across the Wye, and the Norman settlers, as well as with occasional immigrants from elsewhere in the country. It may well be that these various strands are identifiable to some extent in the skeletons as broad trends.

The general effects caused by nutritional and environmental conditions will also be studied. The range of diseases already observed is wide and more can be expected. As would be anticipated, many of the adults—particularly the elderly ones—had problems with their bones. Then, as now, arthritis was prevalent and several cases of osteoporosis were also found. The incidence of DISH, a disease in which the cartilage is calcified to the individual vertebrae of the backbone, joining several together so that the back cannot be bent, may indicate a high protein diet. If so, it is likely to have affected the rich more than the poor. Throughout the period there was little sign of poor nutrition, with only occasional exceptions, such as one case of rickets and a few individuals with enamel hypoplasia (a type of tooth disease).

The average height of adults remained much the same throughout the period. Initial indications are that this population was generally smaller than has been found in other medieval cemeteries (White, 1988, 31). However, in the earlier period the range in stature was noticeably greater. Also, there were indications that at this earlier time people tended to be more muscular than in the post-medieval period. The interim determination of the ages of the skeletons has shown that there were many more adults than children, and only around thirty infants. This conflicts with the well-established belief that half the population died in childhood, though this may be explained by discrete areas being put aside for child burials, as appeared to be the case to the south of the site. There are also indications from other excavations in the city and throughout the country that infants and those still-born were buried in otherwise disused burial grounds to avoid paying fees. The sexes, however, do seem to be roughly evenly represented.

The plant and animal remains give some indication of the range of food eaten. Most of the evidence which has so far been examined came from deposits of eleventh and twelfth century date. The principal cereal crop was barley, with a fair amount of oat supplementing it, and smaller amounts of wheat and other cereals. A narrow range of fruits was available most of which grew locally. Some, such as apples and pears, were cultivated, others were probably wild and included blackberries, elderberries and sloes. Figs, probably imported, were also found.

Hazelnuts would have been a useful source of protein, but the population were also meat eaters. As well as bones of domesticated animals such as cow, sheep and pig, remains of wild animals such as rabbit and deer were found. Venison would have been particularly sought after and was mainly the preserve of the nobles and churchmen as deer were the king's beasts and penalties for illegal hunting were very severe. The several skeletons of cats and dogs were presumably remains of working animals or pets.

Finds from graves were rare as a whole, but barrel padlocks were found in two late Saxon graves. In later periods many nails and a few iron fittings indicate that coffins were in relatively common use although all traces of the wood had disappeared. There were several possible shroud buckles. Ornaments include seven copper alloy rings and hose hooks, dress pins, a brooch pin and several beads. Occasional fragments of textile were found in association with metallic objects, but the general lack of organic materials means that there is little evidence for dress, especially for grave clothing.

Although the cemetery provides little evidence for trading in the area and the loss through lowering of the ground level of the deposits related to the eighteenth century timber yard was particularly unfortunate, it is still possible to build up a picture of the variety of occupations in this part of the city.

There was debris from the working of stone for building, and some of the fragments of the fifteenth century cloister had traces of paintwork. There would have been an extended network of craftsmen involved in building: carpenters, masons, painters, glaziers, plumbers, and labourers. For the major buildings of the city such as the cathedral, castle and Bishop's Palace master craftsmen are likely to have been brought in from elsewhere in the country, but the majority of the labour force would have been local.

An eleventh century iron sword with a pattern-welded blade from the cess pit was one of the more important finds. The hilt was possibly of horn and the wood of the scabbard was of ash. Whether this was of local manufacture is unknown.

Later finds include a book clasp and trap, a harness fitting, spindle whorls, an apothecary bottle, wig curlers and an unusual group of bone apple corers, the last of which were surely of local manufacture and a spin off from the butchery trade.

Ceramics were well represented, particularly in the earlier periods. A large and important group of eleventh and twelfth century pottery was found, including limestone-tempered wares produced in the Cotswolds, and West Midlands Early Medieval Ware. Vessels from Stamford and Winchester were also present. By the late twelfth and early thirteenth centuries, Malvernian wares and Herefordshire jugs were increasingly common. Later periods were, as a whole, poorly represented, although a sixteenth century pit group produced several vessels of interest. From this time on, there was little pottery, probably because it was removed when the ground level was reduced at the time the area was landscaped.

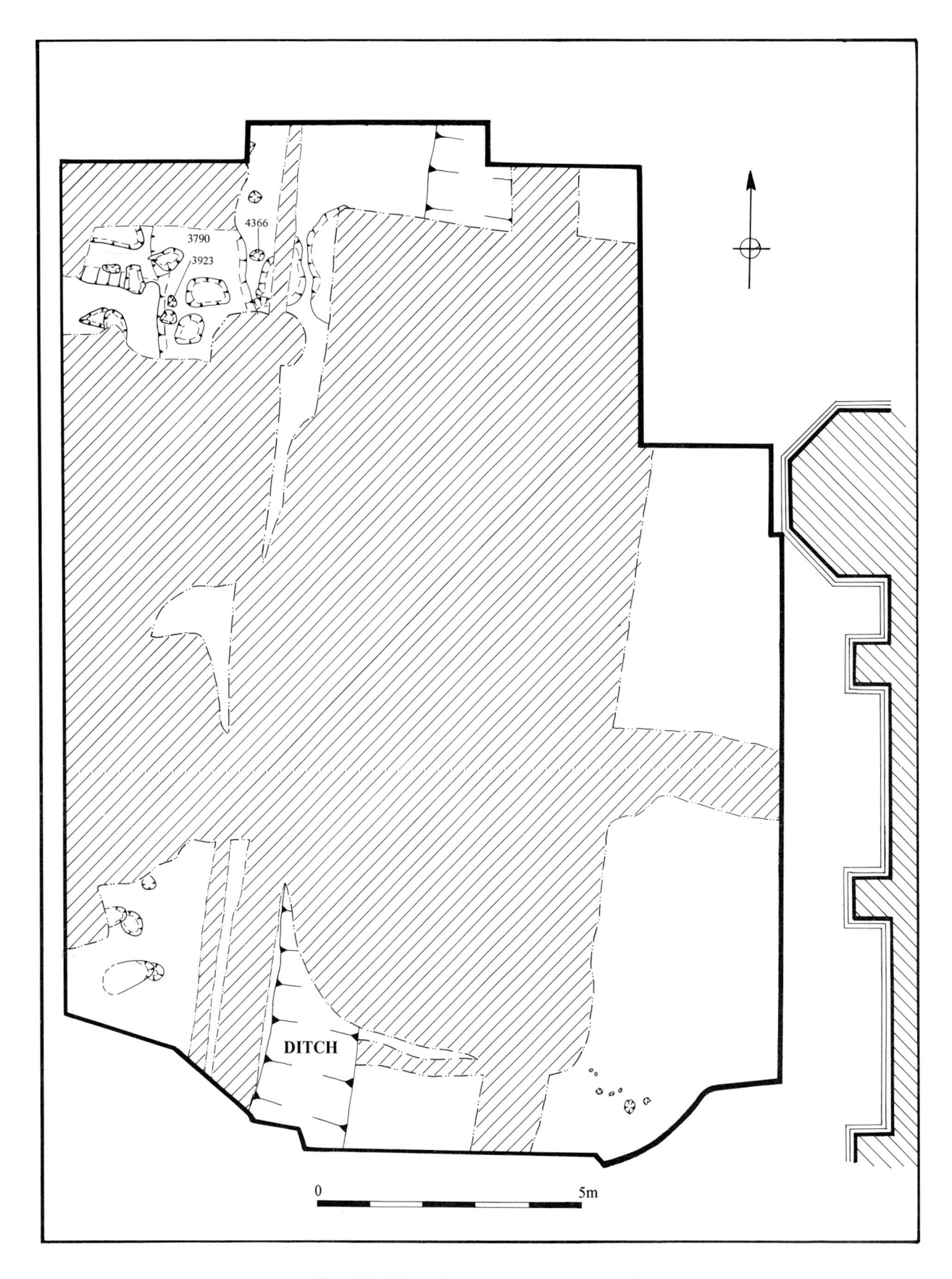

Fig. 16. Plan of the excavation, Period 1

Detailed Description of the Excavation

THE EARLIEST SETTLEMENT (Period 1) (Fig. 16)

Description

Overlying the natural gravels of the river terrace was a partially surviving layer of moderately well-compacted light brown silt loam. A similar layer has been found on several sites in the city and is interpreted as a natural build-up of soil.

This soil layer was much disturbed by later uses of the site but, at the south-west corner, several features were identified indicating some occupation during this period. The largest of these was a north-south ditch in which Roman tile was found. The west side of a similar feature at the extreme north of the excavation had a broadly similar alignment and may be the continuation of this ditch. Several other features produced small amounts of Roman material, almost exclusively ceramic tile. No other datable artefacts were recovered. Other features included a small area at the south-east where twelve stake holes and a post hole were identified. Several of these were below a cobbled surface of late Saxon date, but this was intermittent and it is possible that some of the stakes were of a later date and had cut through the surface.

At the north-west of the site some six square metres of the natural soil accumulation had not been damaged by features of later date and was selected to test the extent of occupation. Nineteen features were identified. Most were very difficult to distinguish, being recognisable only by a slight increase in the content of stones or charcoal and it is possible that some were natural depressions. All the associated deposits were without pottery remains. Amongst the earliest features was a large shallow pit (3790). After this pit had been filled two further pits and a number of post and stake holes were dug in the same area. One of these stake holes (3923) contained some charcoal. This, together with a small pit (4366), filled with charcoal, burnt clay, and slag, suggests some industrial activity in the vicinity.

Discussion

The natural accumulation of buried soil on the site is generally very clean and contains little evidence of human activity. However, more early features were found cutting into it than in most previous excavations in Hereford. These features must relate to the early development of the settlement, but as the material filling them is very similar to the surrounding soil they are difficult to identify. This problem is increased as there is no pottery evidence in Hereford until the middle of the tenth century. This makes dating difficult and reduces the chance of finds. Similar early features have been found on other sites in Hereford (Shoesmith, 1982, 47-53) but detailed examination was not always possible and the density of activity found on this site may well be present in other areas of the city.

The ceramic material from the north-south ditch and other features was all tile of Roman date. This could indicate that the ditch is of Roman origin, but it could equally be of Saxon date, with the tile brought in from elsewhere, possibly *Magnis*, as building material. Radiocarbon dating of the associated animal bone may provide a solution.

The clear evidence in the area tested of intense activity in this early period is compatible with an urban environment. It is unfortunate that the later use of the site destroyed most of the remains of this elusive period and that insufficient remained to establish the overall use of the site.

THE LATE SAXON PERIOD (Period 2) (Fig. 18)

Description

In the eastern part of the site a cobbled layer was sealed by an accumulation of soil that was later cut by several burials dug into the natural gravels. There was a difference in the depth of burial of around 0.8 metres between the bases of the graves of two groups of burials in this area. It is assumed that this represents the division between the late Saxon burials on the one part and those associated with the area's use as part of the period 4 medieval cemetery on the other. Accepting this assumption, there were 21 late Saxon inhumations, all in single graves. Seven were male, seven female, and seven could not be classified. Four juveniles were present, the rest were adults.

Several of the graves cut into or through what must have been earlier burials indicating that at least three 'generations' of burial were present during this period, all in clearly defined rows. All the individuals were buried in the usual Christian posture: supine (face upward), extended and with the head to the west. There was some differentiation in the position of the arms; usually they were placed with the hands in the area of the pelvis or by the sides but two had the arms in other positions. Two of the grave cuts contained patches of black staining, considered to represent remains of wooden coffins. One late Saxon burial practice that was represented was the use of 'pillow' stones, to hold the head in place in the grave, in graves 3832 and 3767. In addition, two burials included iron barrel padlocks, both found by the left pelvis; one of the individuals was an adolescent, the other an adult female (3843 and 4215) (Figs. 17 & 39).

Apart from these, very few objects were recovered from grave fills. One burial (3989) included both a quarter penny, of late eleventh century date, and a fragment of a glass bead; another (3767) had a copper alloy ring and a flint flake; and one (3991) had a single flint flake. However, none of these can be definitely accepted as grave goods.

Although nails were found in six graves, in only one were they sufficient to indicate the presence of a coffin. The soil conditions were such that all wood (except where it was

Fig. 17. Skeleton 3843, with the arms in the pelvic area and a barrel padlock by the left side of the pelvis

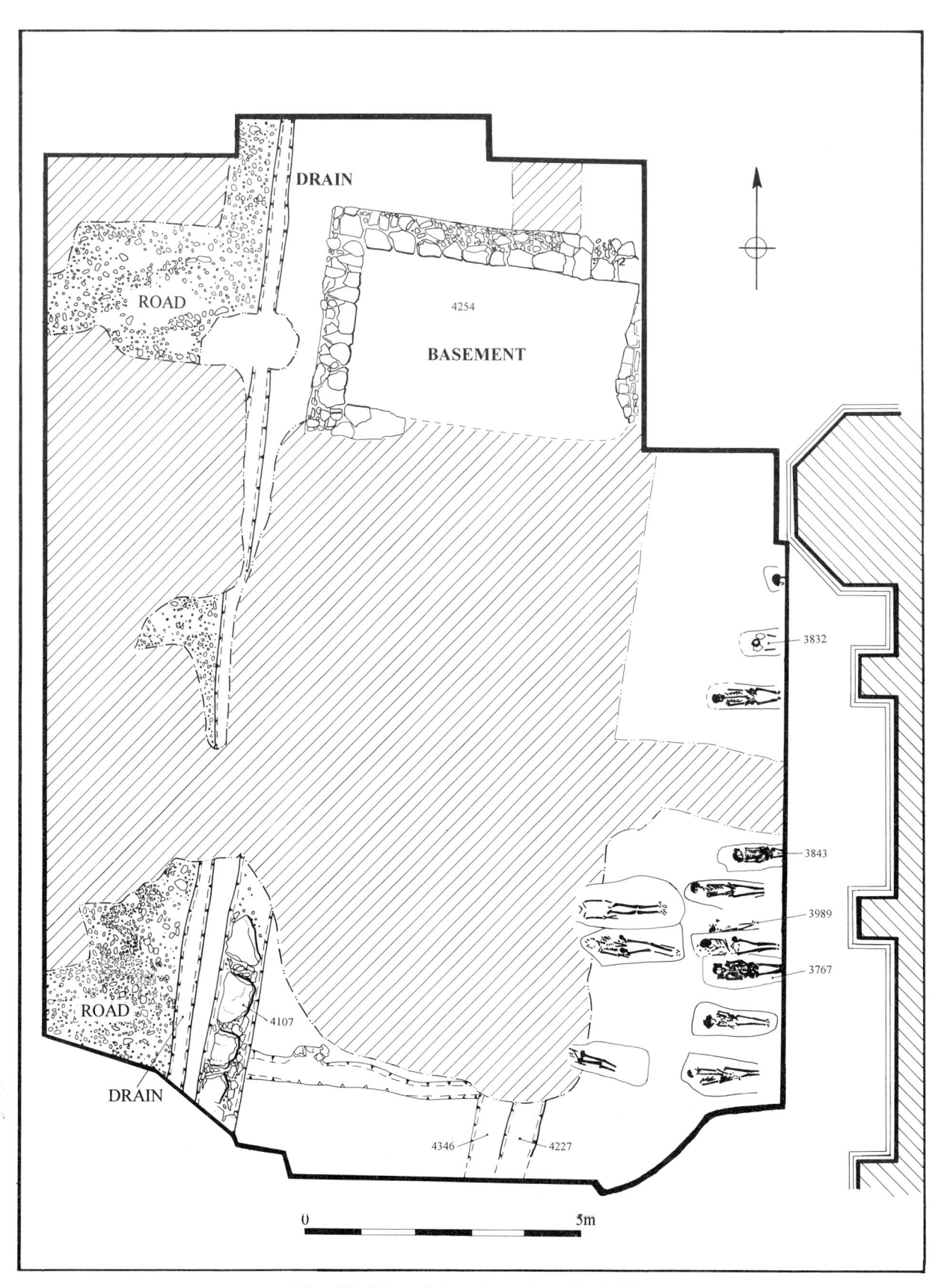

Fig. 18. Plan of the excavation, Period 2
Not all of the burials are shown

charred) and textile had decayed and no traces remained. However, both of the padlocks retained textile impressions on the side nearest the body indicating the former presence, in these graves at least, of some form of garment or shroud.

The burials were densely packed to the east of the area, but became dispersed in the westernmost row. At the south of the site, just to the west of the western row of burials, were two adjacent linear features running nearly north-south (4227 and 4346). Both had almost vertical sides and flat bases, and the easternmost one (4227) may have contained the stone foundation for a wall, later robbed out for use elsewhere. Either of these could represent the western boundary of the cemetery at that time.

Further west, the land use during this period of occupation was very different. Along the whole of the western side of the excavation was a series of cobbled surfaces forming a road (Fig. 12). This road sealed the traces of the earliest settlement and overlay the natural soil of the site. The full width of the road could not be seen in the excavation, but the earliest of the surfaces extended 4 metres from the western edge of the excavation. At a later date a trench filled with graded stones was dug through the eastern edge of this surface. It was 0.3 metres wide and deep, with straight sides. The trench continued for the full length of the excavation, sloping down towards the south. It followed a similar alignment to the suggested boundary of the cemetery. Subsequent re-surfacings of the road with cobbles were limited on the east by this stone-filled trench, which was probably a drain at the side of the road.

Between the road and the cemetery were the stone foundations of two masonry structures aligned with the presumed drain.

The southern of these, towards the south of the site, was a half metre deep foundation trench 0.65 metres wide (4107) (Fig. 19). The foundation itself consisted of large blocks of local sandstone with an average dimension of 0.4 metres in the middle of the trench, packed on both sides with smaller, angular fragments of sandstone. The foundation trench extended beyond the southern limit of the excavation and to the north it was cut by a later pit.

To the east of the foundation trench there was a gravel surface (4058) which was much worn and petered out after a metre. Above it was an accumulation of occupation debris that may indicate an open yard or a room within a building.

Fig. 19. Foundation trench 4107

Fig. 20. The stone-lined basement 4254

The two trenches (4227 & 4346), previously described as possible boundaries for the cemetery, were approximately 5 metres east of this foundation trench and ran parallel to it. An alternative hypothesis is that one or both could be associated with a building of which 4107 would represent the front wall. In that case the westernmost trench may be the foundation trench for the rear wall of the building.

In the northern part of the site was the other masonry structure. This was a stone-lined basement (4254) 5.1 metres by 2.75 metres internally with stonework surviving for a maximum height of 2.85 metres (Fig. 20). This basement had been dug into the natural gravels and was built of roughly-coursed local sandstone, the walls being 0.65 metres thick. The stones were laid against the vertical edge of the gravel cut, with rubble corework behind the fair face. The whole was bonded with a fairly strong mortar. There was no evidence to indicate that the walls had ever been plastered. The floor of the basement consisted of a thick impermeable deposit of mortar of different composition to that used in the walls. There were no features in the masonry to indicate where there may have been timberwork, such as might be expected for steps or floor joists. The upper part of the west wall was of slightly different character to the rest and may have been re-built.

The sequence of layers directly outside the basement indicated that all the surviving masonry of this building was below the contemporary ground level. However, as the basement was contemporary with the cobbled surface to its west, the uppermost parts were probably very close to floor level. To the north of the basement was a series of 18 stake holes, perhaps reflecting a fence line.

Above the mortar floor of the basement there was a half metre thick deposit of organic material, containing thin layers of ash, charcoal, lime and soil. The majority of the build-up was tinged green and this, together with the presence of coprolites and a high level of mineralisation of plant remains, indicates that the basement had been used as a cesspit or latrine.

There were relatively few man-made artefacts within this midden material. However, a pattern-welded sword of late Saxon date, complete with its scabbard, was found near the bottom of the deposit. There was also a large amount of animal bone, indicating that organic waste had been dumped in the basement, and two complete skeletons of dogs and two of cats (Fig. 21).

Fig. 21. Skeletons of two dogs in the late Saxon cesspit

The few pottery sherds found indicate that this period continued until the end of the eleventh century, whilst the almost total lack of tenth century material suggests a start in the early eleventh century.

Discussion

The occupation of the site during the eleventh century is divided into two different areas of land use: the cemetery to the east and the road and building(s) to the west.

The cemetery

The excavated Saxon burials were in a part of the cemetery associated with the early cathedral, much of the remainder of which would have been disturbed by the construction of the new Norman cathedral. The presence of at least three generations of burials on the site suggests that this part of the graveyard had been in use for a minimum of 90 years, allowing thirty years per generation. With the exception of the two individuals who were buried with padlocks (perhaps part of a trousseau or chatelaine), the normal Christian burial practice was followed, with the body laid on its back in an individual grave with the head to the west with the legs extended and without grave goods.

The small patches of blackened timber may have resulted from the deliberate charring of coffins. This was sometimes done at this time to reduce the smell of decay and to lessen the risk of infection. Seven iron nails were found in one grave, again suggesting the presence of a coffin. These examples were the only cases providing evidence to indicate that a coffin was used. On Castle Green, most of the burials considered to be later than 1000AD were without any trace of coffins, although the presence of nails was quite common before that date. There were also two examples of the Saxon practice of burying the body with the head supported by 'pillow' stones, but no trace of charcoal burials (where the body was laid on a bed of charcoal within the grave) such as occurred at Castle Green in the ninth and tenth centuries (Shoesmith, 1980, 25-27) and which are often found in late Saxon cemeteries (Richards, 1991, 110).

The road frontage
The cemetery extended right up to the back wall of at least one of the houses that fronted onto the roadway—that with a stone-lined basement. The area immediately to the south of this building had been dug away at a later date, destroying any evidence that there may have been for further buildings.

Accepting that it was disused before the beginning of the twelfth century, this building is most unusual. There are no known parallels for a house with a stone-built basement at this date. The above ground building would either have been of stone or of timber on a stone cill. The thickness of the basement walls would allow for a two-storey timber building (Fig. 11) or a single storey of stone, but all above ground evidence is lacking and the reconstruction of a building above basement level has to be hypothetical.

There is insufficient evidence to provide an accurate date for the construction of the house with the basement. It could be purely Saxon but could equally reflect the Norman influence in Hereford and date to the end of the Saxon period or to the first years after the Norman Conquest. The location may well indicate that it was owned by the cathedral and rented out, perhaps to a merchant, with the basement being designed for use as a warehouse. If this was the case it would argue for an earlier date of construction, as the main market place at the Broad Street/King Street cross-roads in the Saxon period was moved to High Town, outside the city walls, shortly after 1067. Before the Conquest the frontages along such a major axial road are certainly likely to have been desirable properties.

An alternative explanation is that the basement and wall to the south are both part of an earlier Bishop's Palace. The earliest surviving part of the present palace shares this alignment and is dated to the later twelfth century, nearly 100 years after the use of the basement as a cesspit. However, the foundations to the south (4107) may not have been part of a building but a boundary wall. In that case the basement could have formed part of a gatehouse leading into the cathedral precinct. Had a wall been found continuing north beyond the basement as a precinct boundary this interpretation would have been more likely. Other suggestions that have been made include the use of the building as a church or mausoleum. The alignment, broadly east-west, would fit, but the building would have been quite small for such a use and there is no additional evidence to support an ecclesiastical function, so this is unlikely.

Some time after it was built the use of the basement changed radically. The mortar floor was covered in a thick layer of faecal material and general refuse. Towards the bottom of these deposits was the pattern-welded sword that has been dated to the mid-eleventh century. Whilst it is possible that it was dumped there with the refuse, it is perhaps more likely that the sword was dropped into the cesspit and sank to the bottom.

The presence of an impermeable mortar floor, which would have inhibited the run off from the cesspit, indicates that it was not the basement's primary use. Later slumping of part of the medieval cemetery into the upper part of the basement indicates that the material in the cesspit gradually became more compacted. It is suggested that it was originally over a metre deep.

The possible second building to the south is even more difficult to interpret as the stratigraphic sequence is unclear. It is possible that one of the narrower trenches, excavated just to the west of the burials, represents the rear wall of a building fronting onto the road. If this is the case, then the building would have extended back from the road for a similar distance as the building with the basement. The suggested foundation trenches for the rear wall were narrower than those of the front wall, suggesting that the rear wall was of timber, perhaps with a stone frontage to the road. Because of the damage caused by later features and the continuation of the stone foundation to the south of the excavation, the width of such a building is uncertain. Alternatively, it may be that the wall simply enclosed a yard adjoining the western limit of the cathedral precinct.

However, there is yet another possible interpretation. It may be that the eastern trenches were not associated at all with the large foundation trench fronting onto the road. In that case the latter may have extended northwards to join with the south side of the northern building, thus forming a boundary wall. This is, however, unlikely since the rear of the southern wall of the basement was entirely of coarse core material, whereas had there been an extension to the south it would probably have included face material.

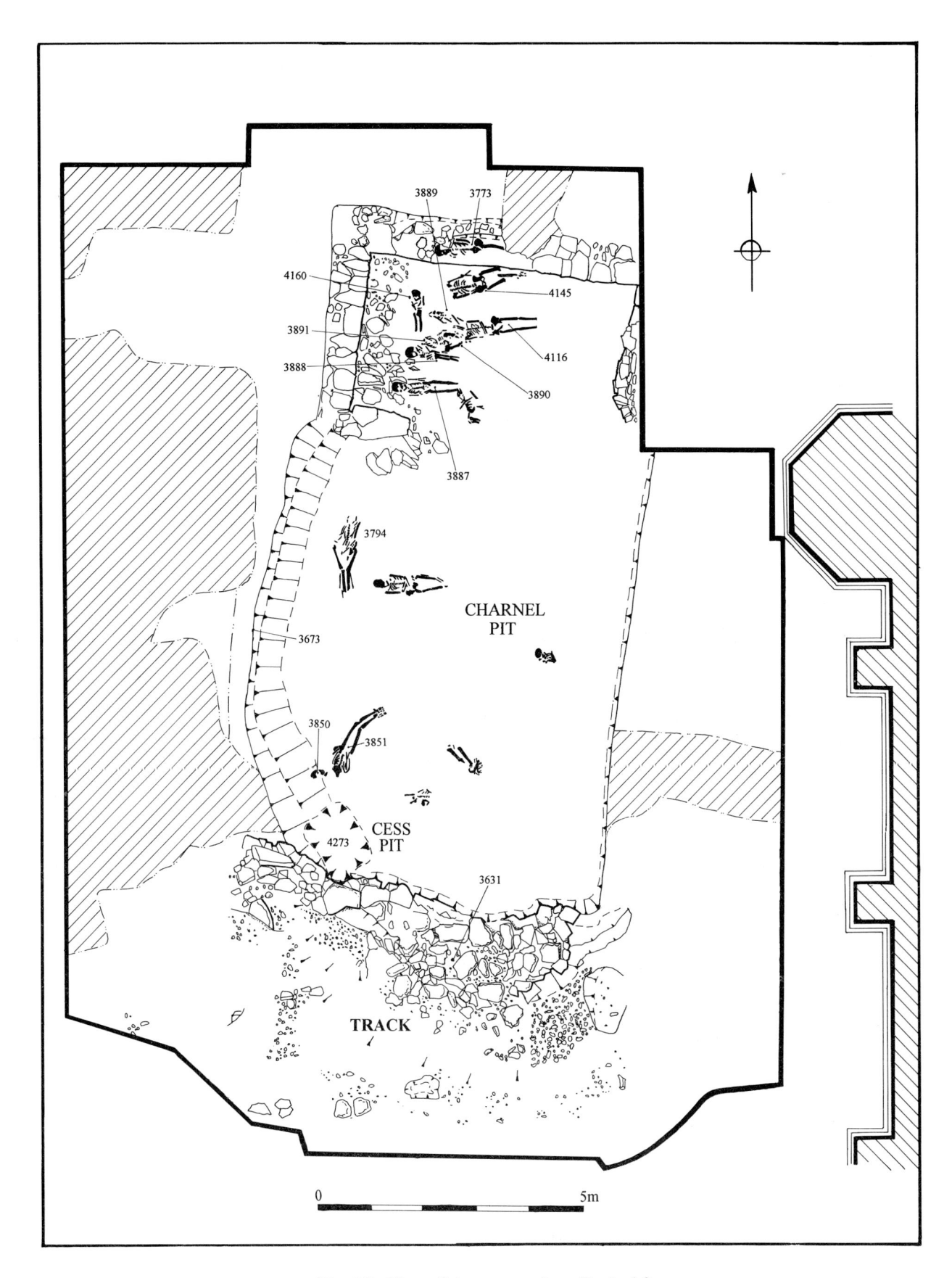

Fig. 22. Plan of the excavation, Period 3

THE GRAVEL QUARRY & CHARNEL PIT (Period 3) (Fig. 22)

Description

The largest feature found during the excavation was a sub-rectangular pit (3673) that had been excavated in the centre of the site, presumably for extracting gravel. It cut through and partly destroyed many of the major features of the late Saxon period, including the burials on its eastern side, the basement to its north, the foundation to the south, and the roadside drain on its western side. Its maximum length was 11 metres north to south, whilst it measured 7 metres wide for much of its length. When the excavation started it had been assumed that all archaeological levels would be above the level needed for the new basement, but this pit extended below that level and the lower fill could be left in place. However, on completion of the formal excavation, a 3 metre wide east-west trench was excavated by mechanical digger to the bottom of the pit, which was found to be some 4.75 metres below the present ground level. Elsewhere, the pit-fill material below the level required for the new basement was left *in situ*.

The sides of the pit were irregular but generally almost vertical. However, at the eastern side a shallow slope continued beyond the confines of the main pit and at the south the soil and underlying gravels were cut back to form steps into the pit. There was no trace of any lining to the pit.

A substantial amount of the walling of the late Saxon basement was removed, probably when the pit was dug, including the whole of the south wall, except for a small section at the south-west corner. A small amount of the west wall was also taken down, and the upper parts of the north and east walls were removed to an increasing depth towards the east. This left the north-west corner at full height but the north-east corner at only about half height.

In the south-west corner of the pit, close to the steps leading down into it, was a sub-rectangular cesspit (4273), 1.25 metres by 1 metre and 2.35 metres deep, which was filled with environmentally rich material. Although it is possible that the cesspit was dug in the late Saxon period (period 2), the fill of the upper part of it was the same material as that in the gravel pit, so it is likely that they were both open at the same time.

The gravel pit fill continued northwards to include the upper part of the stone-lined basement.

Fig. 23. Skeleton 4116, with pillow stones

It consisted of mixed layers of human bone and soil (Fig. 14). These layers were present to a total depth of 2.3 metres in the centre of the pit, and 3.3 metres at the edges. Almost all of the human remains were disarticulated. During the excavation, two samples from the fill were examined in detail in an attempt to quantify the whole. From this it has been estimated that about 5,000 individuals were represented in the total deposit. This immense quantity of human material was well beyond the resources of the excavation to process and it was decided that half of the excavated material should be reinterred without any further examination.

The human remains were present to a much higher level at the edges of the pit and, although much of this is doubtless a result of settlement of the material in the central, deeper part of the pit, it also reflects the dumping of the remains into the former gravel quarry from all sides, probably directly from carts.

Only in one area was there any indication that there had been any prior sorting of the remains. This was towards the south-west of the pit, where there was a group of about twenty skulls. Elsewhere the bones were randomly deposited. In the samples studied it appeared that the smaller bones of the body were under-represented in the pit fill.

In addition to the disarticulated remains, 23 partially or fully articulated skeletons were present within the pit fill. Twelve of these were children, all under ten years old. Of the adults, three were definitely female and four male. One skeleton (3773) lay on top of the partially robbed north wall of the late Saxon basement, oriented west-east but covered with further random human bones. The remainder of the articulated skeletons all lay within the deposits of bone. Several consisted of parts of corpses, presumably ones that had been interred elsewhere and redeposited before the ligaments had fully decayed. The majority, however, were complete skeletons, and presumably represent primary interments.

Within the area of the late Saxon basement most of the complete skeletons were correctly oriented. At the western end of the basement were five children (3887-3891) covering a sixth, incorrectly oriented, child (4160). Further east was an adult (4116), laid out with two pillow stones (Fig. 23). Nearby was a skeleton laid facing downwards (4145), missing its head and lower legs. This is likely to have been the re-burial of a decaying corpse (Fig. 24).

South of the basement, towards the centre of the former gravel pit, the orientation was more random. One body (3794), lying north-south, had apparently been rolled in from the west and, slightly further to

Fig. 24. Skeleton 4145, lying prone

the south, another body (3851) was lying on the slope of the previously tipped bone. As the material had settled the angle had become steeper and the head (3850) had eventually become separated from the rest of the body (Fig. 25).

When all the human remains had been deposited, soil was used to fill the pit. This covered the human remains for a depth of up to 1.8 metres in the centre of the pit. This soil was a heterogeneous mixture of silt, loam and gravel that contained a quantity of human bone. The vast majority of these skeletal remains consisted of the smaller bones of the body, together with small fragments of the larger bones.

Above the southern end of the gravel pit was a thick layer of large stones (3631) 9 metres from east to west and 3 metres wide. This overlay the earliest part of the fill of the pit, but may have been laid whilst the backfilling was taking place. It was 0.9 metres deep at the north and 0.5 metres at the south, presumably to achieve a level surface over the sloping fill.

Subsequently, the material in the pit settled and the ground was built up on two further occasions (Fig. 26). The first levelling was only undertaken in the centre of the pit and consisted of several large stones which were then surrounded by a silty soil placed over a diameter of 4 metres. The later campaign was more extensive, covering the whole of the area of the pit (Fig. 27). This involved the use of a quantity of angular fragments of sandstone, perhaps derived from masons' chippings, which were placed up to half a metre deep in the centre of the pit, petering out towards the edges.

Fig. 25. Skeleton 3851, with separated skull 3850

Discussion

The excavation of the large pit clearly represented a sudden, major alteration of the land use. There was no evidence for any collapse of the sides of the pit so it is likely that, although the natural gravels forming the sides were quite well compacted, the pit was only open for a relatively short period. It is suggested that its purpose was for gravel extraction to provide materials for the new cathedral, but why choose this particular spot, containing a building, with a basement, of obviously fairly high status, and possibly others? Was this the only site available which belonged to the cathedral authorities? Was it used because it was close to the construction site for the new building or was it a deliberate insult to the Saxon authori-

*Fig. 26. (top) Slumping of the backfill of the charnel pit from the south,
with the period 5 foundation trench 0048 cut through it*
Fig. 27. (bottom) The two campaigns of levelling up as a result of the slumping of the pit

ties by the new Norman hierarchy? Whatever the reason, the implication is that the site had lost its importance, presumably as a result of the establishment of the new market place shortly after 1067.

The removal of the stonework of the basement probably took place after the gravel had been extracted from the pit, indicating a deliberate effort to obtain serviceable stone. The depth at which the robbing stopped on the north and east sides was presumably just above the original top of the cesspit deposits in the pit. Almost certainly the use of the basement as a cesspit had ceased before the stone was robbed out and probably before the gravel pit was dug.

It is possible that the stone derived from the robbing of the basement masonry was used to construct the east-west surface at the southern end of the pit. This was a substantial effort to form a track leading east from the late Saxon road, possibly servicing a masons' yard.

The ceramic material found in the fill of the gravel pit is dated to around 1100. This should be treated as a *terminus post quem* as, given the depositional process, the artefacts could all be residual.

The disarticulated remains of over 5,000 individuals must have come from from the clearance of a substantial part of a cemetery or from a charnel house, or both. The presence of a significant amount of skeletal material in the upper soil fill suggests that the material was derived from a graveyard clearance, although the group of twenty skulls could equally well be from an ossuary. The most likely source of this material would be from the excavations for the foundation trenches and floors of the Norman replacement of the Saxon cathedral, undertaken by Bishop Reynhelm at the beginning of the twelfth century. The siting of the new cathedral clearly paid little or no attention to the presence of the earlier cemetery.

The backfilling of the quarry pit with the human bone and graveyard soil would have taken a relatively short period of time. Of the 23 fully or partially articulated skeletons recovered from the charnel, over half were under ten years old. Five of these were buried together and were correctly aligned, suggesting that this was their primary place of interment. Some of the others which were incorrectly aligned were almost certainly partly decayed bodies brought from the cemetery. There was evidently some difference in the regard held for the burial of different individuals in this large pit.

After the human bone had been deposited in the pit it was backfilled with a two metre thick layer of soil. This contained a large number of the smaller bones of the body, under-represented in the charnel itself, and small fragments of larger bones. This was probably part of the grave soil from the cleared cemetery which had been roughly sorted when excavated to ensure that the larger human bones were deeply buried. Over time the soil settled and a large depression that appeared had to be levelled on two occasions. By the time of the second levelling the trackway at the south of the pit had been covered over and the north-south road at the west of the site had either become redundant or its line had been moved further to the west, and outside the area excavated. It is likely that once the pit had been completely filled the ground level was raised by using soil brought from elsewhere.

THE MEDIEVAL CEMETERY (Period 4) (Figs. 28, 31 & 33)

Description

After the pit had been completely filled and the ground levelled, the whole area became part of the cathedral cemetery. The inhumations were densely packed, with 1,085 burials being excavated. Of the adults, 215 have been identified as female and 187 as male. 225 were identified as children. There were three pits used as mass graves, from which 189 of the skeletons were excavated. Apart from those buried in mass graves, almost all the burials followed the usual Christian practice of being laid west-east, supine and extended, and in single graves.

The earliest of the burials (Fig. 28) were cut into the stone levelling of the infilled gravel pit, and to a similar depth elsewhere on the site. The high degree of intercutting of all the burials above these, coupled with the reduction of the ground level that took place in 1851, resulted in the removal of all traces of the contemporary ground level. Occasional sherds of pottery in the graves indicates that burial had begun in this area by the thirteenth century.

Several of the earliest burials were within stone-lined graves and one included a pillow stone (as in the late Saxon period). In one case (3008) the lining was continuous around the entire grave and included

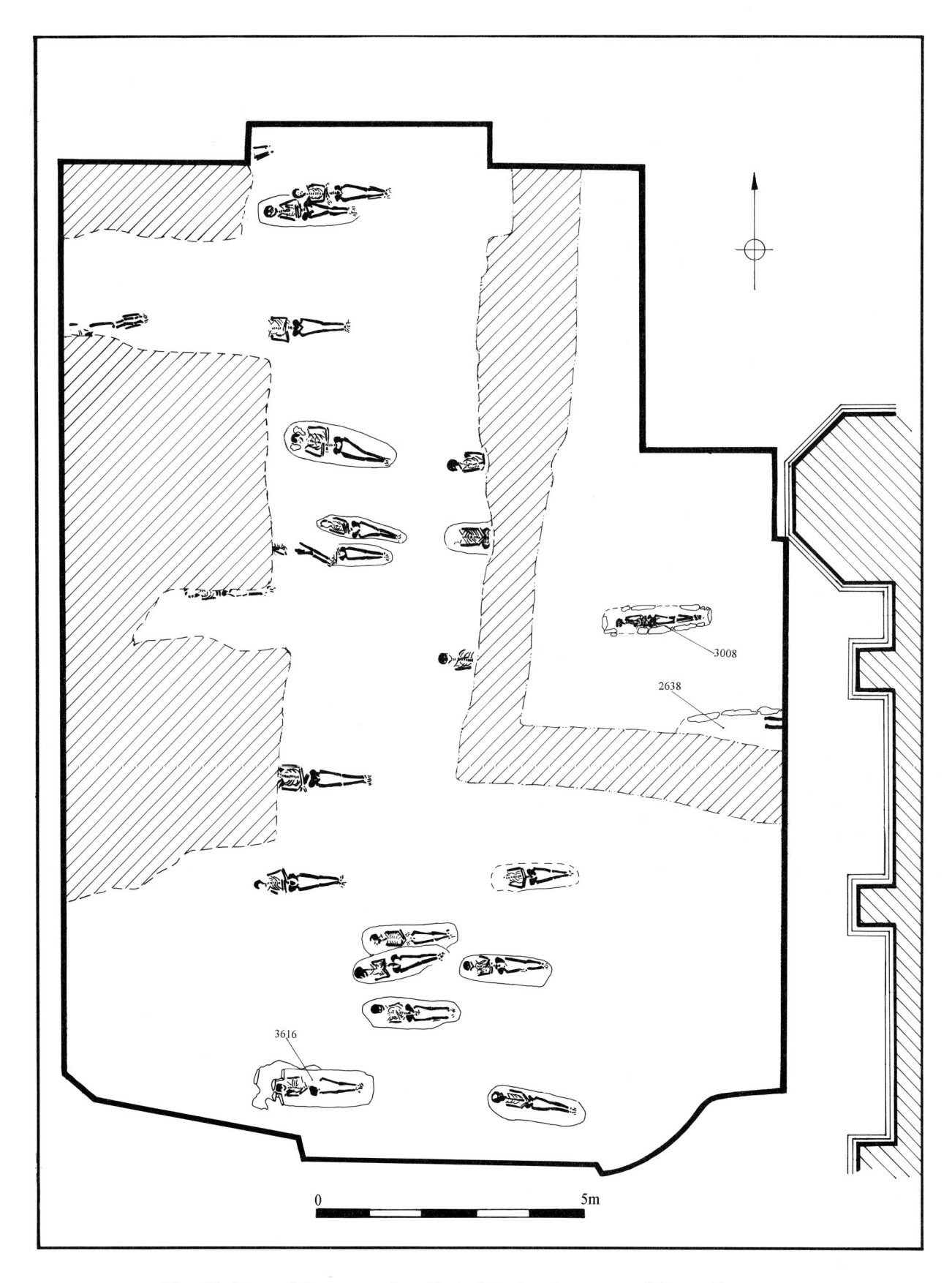

Fig. 28. Plan of the excavation, Period 4, showing some of the earlier graves

capping stones (Fig. 29). A second (2638) may have had a similarly complete lining, but had been truncated at the south. More commonly the lining was intermittent, most frequently with stones concentrated around the head. In one case (3616) a substantial mortar spread directly west of a stone lining may have formed a foundation for an upstanding monument (Fig. 30). One lining stone from grave 3008 had an incised X, and at least one other stone from the same grave may have been reused for it had a chamfered edge. This method of interment using stones soon declined and was not present in later burials.

As with the late Saxon period, the soil conditions were not conducive to survival of organic materials and if coffins were held together with wooden pegs they have decayed entirely. The density of burials and the high level of intercutting made it difficult at times to correlate iron nails (presumably mainly from coffins) with individual burials. However, the use of coffins may be tentatively inferred from specific body positions which imply that the body was not tightly wrapped in a shroud. Such evidence includes dropped jaws and asymmetrical arm positions.

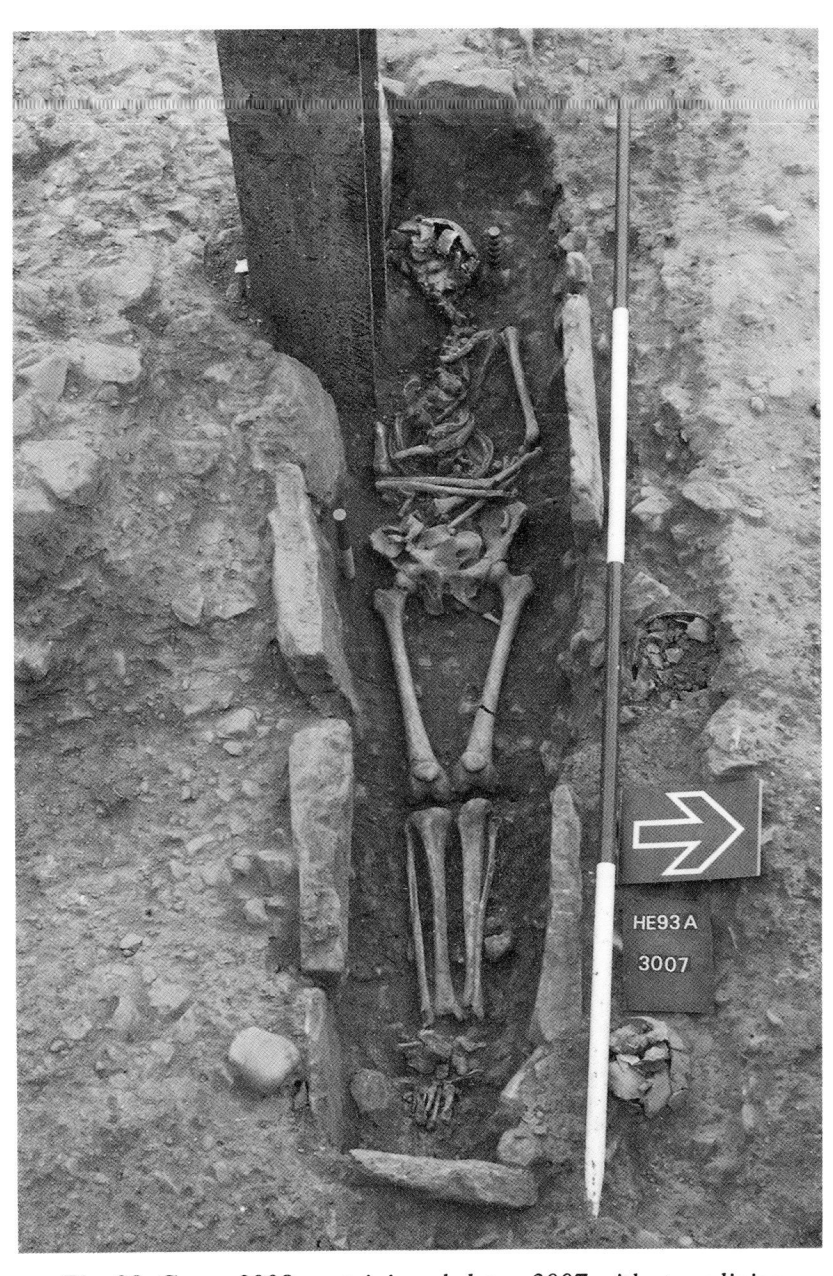

Fig. 29. Grave 3008 containing skeleton 3007 with stone lining, after the removal of the stone capping

There is also the displacement of bones at the base of graves, perhaps due to movement after liquefaction ('bone float'). A cursory appraisal of this information indicates that coffined burials were more common towards the end of the period. Because of the difficulties involved, no attempt has yet been made to quantify the proportion of coffined burials to the whole.

After the cemetery had been in use for some time three pits (0157, 1360, 2359) were dug in a line at the west of the site for the rapid burial of large numbers of individuals (Fig. 31). These pits cut through earlier burials and all three extended to the west of the area excavated, whilst one also extended further north. All had been cut away on the west by later features so the total number of interments clearly exceeded the 189 recorded. The southernmost pit had an irregular southern edge, where the gravediggers had encountered the hard surface of the east-west track (Fig. 15).

The pits had been filled in rough horizontal layers. Some soil was present, and there were several consecutive dumps of a clayey soil between 20mm and 100mm thick separating groups of inhumations. The pottery indicates a date between the late fourteenth and mid fifteenth centuries for these mass graves.

The majority of the burials in the mass graves were laid supine, extended and were oriented west-east. Some were in coffins, as in the rest of the cemetery. However, a small number were poorly oriented or flexed. This was particularly frequent in the southernmost pit (1360) (Fig. 15), where one corpse (2926) was laid east-west, another north-south (3024) and a third south-north (2994). In the central mass grave, (0157), one burial (1691) had fully flexed legs (Fig. 32), another slightly flexed (2127). In the northern pit (2359), two individuals were laid east-west (2954; 2969). Because of the several layers of burial in each pit, not all these burials are apparent in Fig. 31.

After the mass graves had been completely filled, the area they occupied ceased to be used as part of the general cemetery, although the rest of the excavated site continued to be used as a normal graveyard well into the sixteenth century (Fig. 33).

Besides the mass graves, a number of graves contained double burials. Although these usually involved an adult and a child, at least one was of two adults (0597 and 0632), and one was a pregnant woman, with the child in breech position (3409 and 3410) (Fig. 34).

Fig. 30. Skeleton 3616, with a spread of mortar, perhaps a foundation for a monument, to the west

It is clear from the large degree of intercutting that many more bodies were interred and that some have subsequently been entirely removed as a result of the later lowering of the whole area. With the exception of those in the mass grave pits, dug to a depth of 1.5 metres, all the burials of this period were within a metre of the present ground surface, and the majority within 0.7 metres. The uppermost were less than 100mm below the surface. A drainage trench south of the main excavation revealed the remains of 12 children and no adults. The preliminary analysis of the stratigraphic sequence has indicated that in most parts of the site there were between five and ten 'generations' of burials, whilst in the densest areas there were at least 15 'generations'.

Discussion

The earlier graves

According to the pottery evidence it was some time after the backfilling of the quarry pit before the area was again used as a cemetery, probably around the middle of the thirteenth century. The earliest interments had been laid in graves that were only 0.3 metres deep below the ground level when the gravel pit

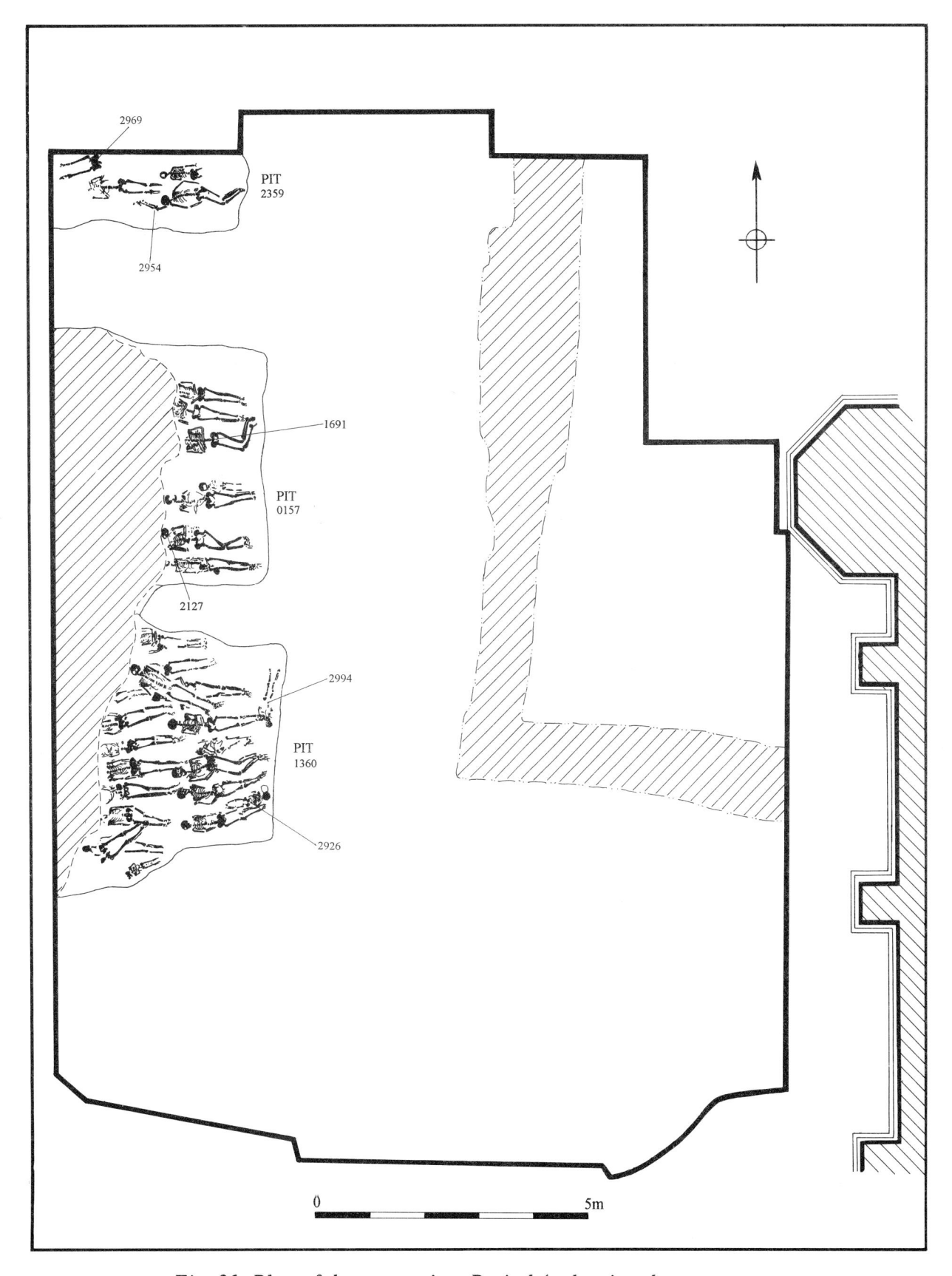

Fig. 31. Plan of the excavation, Period 4, showing the mass graves

was infilled. It is unlikely that they were buried at such a shallow depth and it is probable that by this time a substantial layer of soil had been deliberately deposited on the site. The area may well not have been used for some time because of the mass grave beneath, or perhaps because there was no pressure on space until the thirteenth century. Certainly, the area had been used for several 'generations' of burials before the fill in the basement subsided. Several skeletons which had been buried over the edges of the basement wall had sheared, with the portions inside having dropped by up to 0.5 metres as the cesspit fill gradually settled.

The mass graves

The three mass graves were all dug with their eastern edges in alignment, possibly marking the position of a path, but certainly indicating that they were contemporary. Although none of them fell totally within the area of the excavation, and all had been cut by later features, they produced 189 skeletons. The total number in these pits alone must, therefore, have been in excess of 300, and there could well be further mass graves to the north. This is a large number of deaths for a community of perhaps 3,000, the likely population of Hereford at that time. This method of burial, in a Christian context, must be interpreted as a result of some catastrophe. The burials did not exhibit shared pathologies and it is considered that the individuals died over a period of several weeks or months as a result of a severe epidemic. The specific disease has not been established but, as the pottery from these pits indicates a date between the late-fourteenth and mid-fifteenth centuries, the Black Death is the most likely candidate for the cause of death. The bubonic plague arrived in Hereford in 1349 and returned in 1361-2. It has been suggested that the population of Hereford dropped from some 3,000 to about 1,000 as a result of this double visitation. (Shoesmith, 1992, 44).

The arrangement of the skeletons in pit 0157 demonstrates the method of interment in what were obviously unusual circumstances. A number of bodies were first laid in the pit and were then covered by a thin layer of clay-rich soil. A further layer of burials followed. The dumping of soil between each group of inhumations may represent an attempt to prevent the worst of the smell and to minimise the risk of infection. The presence of several of these layers, producing what has been called a 'lasagne' effect,

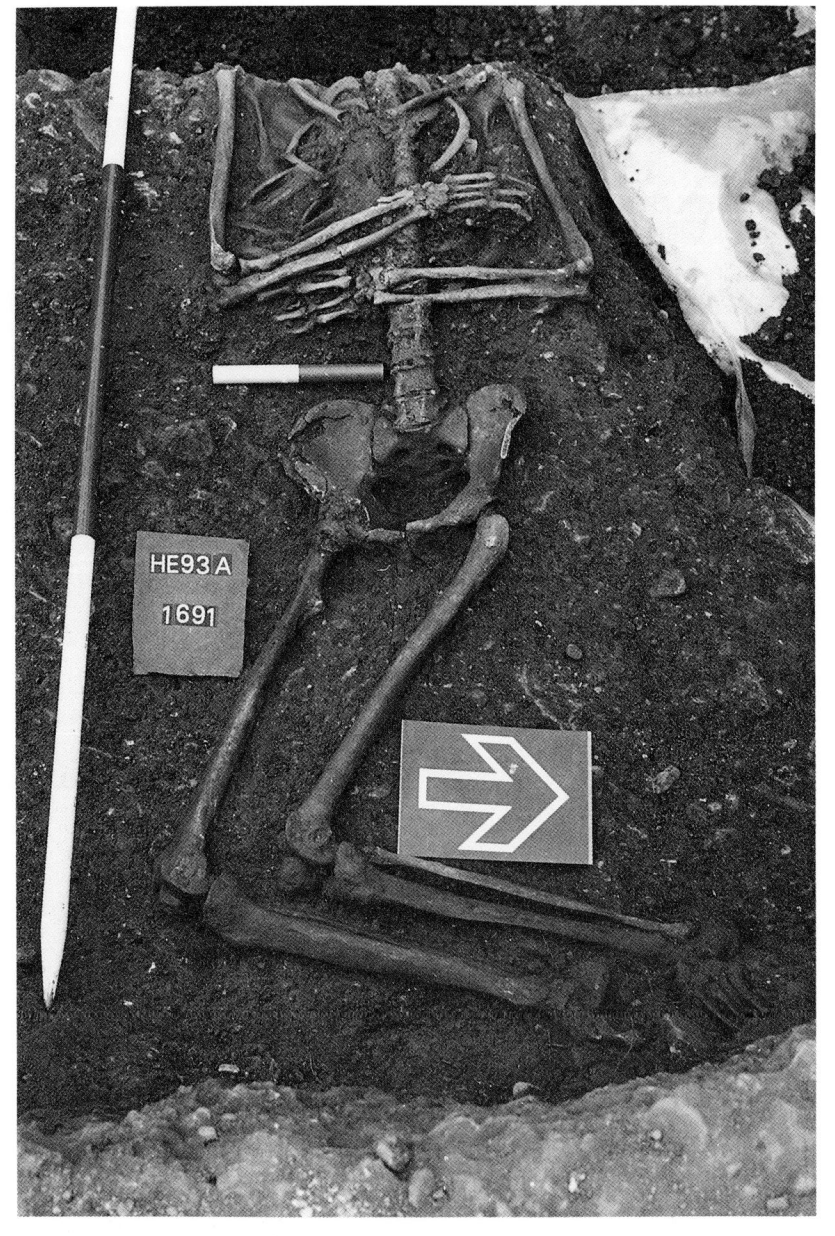

Fig. 32. Flexed skeleton (1691) in the central mass grave

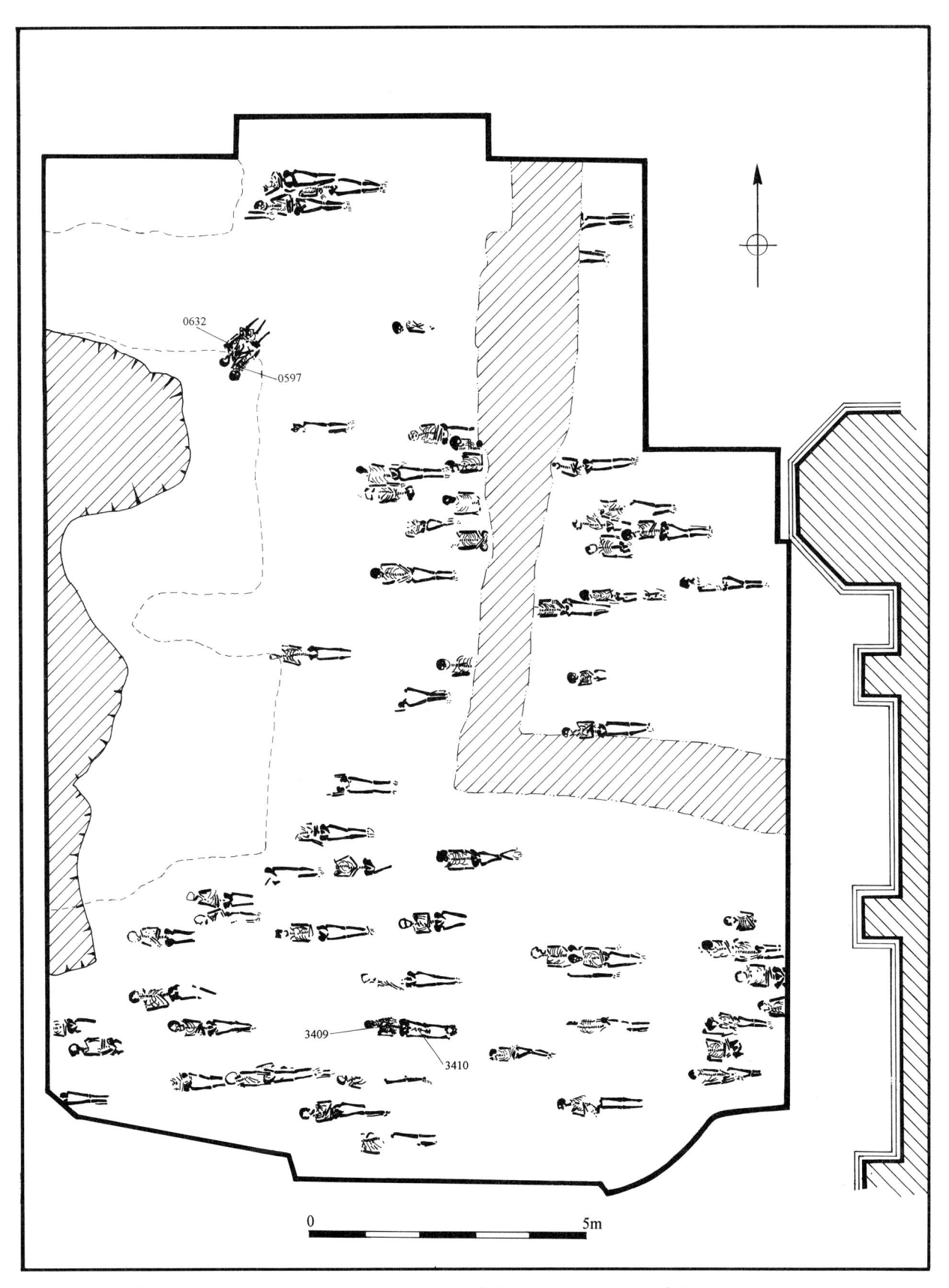

Fig. 33. Plan of the excavation, Period 4, showing some of the later burials and the avoidance of the area of the mass graves

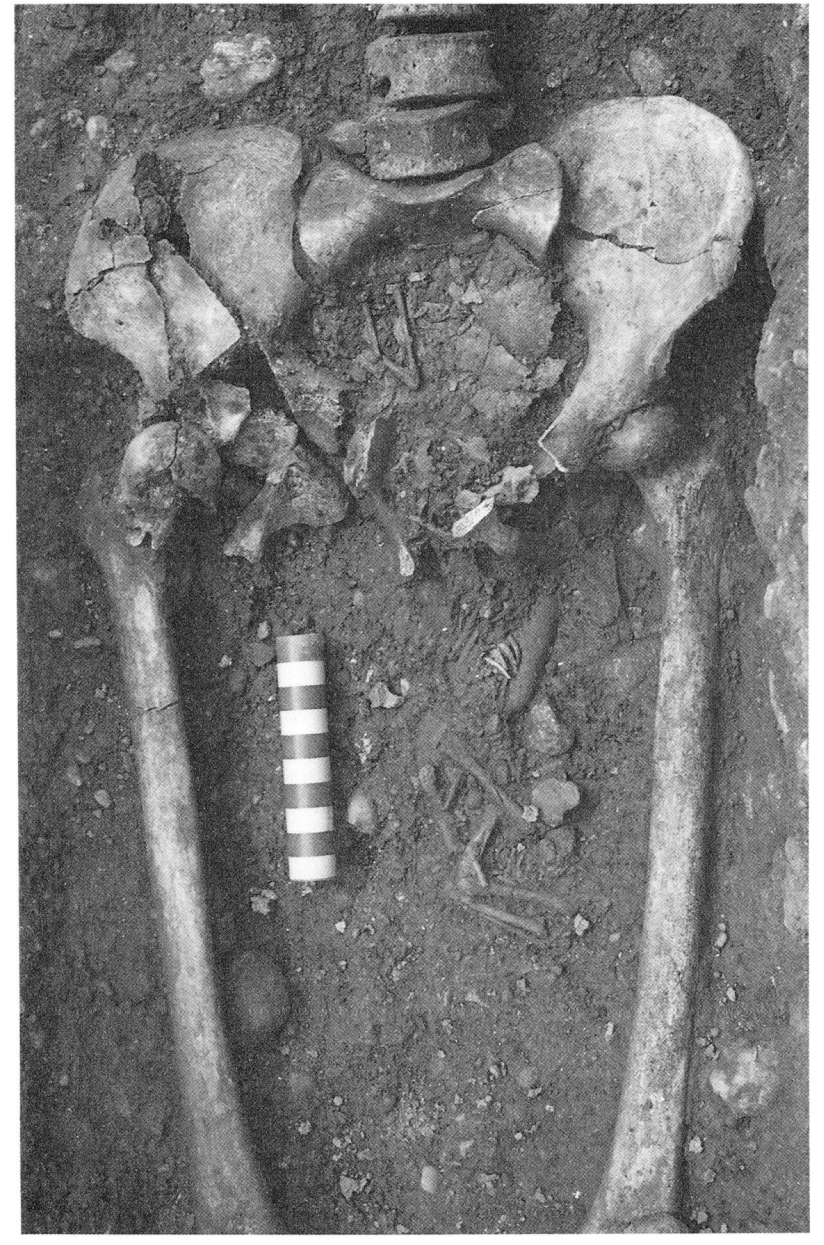

Fig. 34. Detail of foetus 3410 and the mother 3409

tends to indicate that the pits were open for a period of at least several days with a clay capping laid at the end of each working day. The pits were probably dug successively rather than all being in use at one time.

Some of the skeletons within the pits showed signs of decomposition before interment. This was particularly marked in the most southerly pit, 2359, which also was the most densely packed. One particular group on the northern edge of this pit all showed signs of 'bone float'; perhaps they were bodies that had come into the city on a cart from an outlying parish. It is likely that this pit was dug at the height of the epidemic as every available space was used to pack in the bodies. Small children were tucked into the spaces around the edge with no respect for the standard west-east Christian alignment.

As this part of the graveyard was never again used for burial, there may well have been some form of monument or other marker to indicate the position of the mass graves. Had this been so, all traces would have been removed when the ground surface was lowered in 1851.

Other medieval burial practices

Apart from the mass graves, the cemetery produced examples of a variety of burial practices. Some of these reflect the different social status of the deceased, others the changes in practice over time. As there were fifteen 'generations' of burials overlying each other the sequence of the changes can be determined, if not their absolute dates.

All the burials from the general cemetery area were broadly orientated in the standard Christian west-east axis, with the exception of two that were mysteriously reversed, both in the same locality. There were, however, several variants in burial position, all involving different positions of the arms. The preferred form of burial during the Saxon period had been with the arms crossed and resting on the pelvis. Over time the preferred position changed until, probably by the thirteenth century, the arms were folded across the stomach (Fig. 35). Later the normal position changed to having the arms crossed over the chest (Fig. 36). The latest burials tended to show more random arm positions probably due to the bodies being buried in coffins. Other variations include one arm by the side and one across the stomach, and both arms by the side and arms crossed over the chest with the hands resting on the shoulders. Some of these may not have been deliberate arrangements, the arms could have slumped out of place during or after deposition. There were

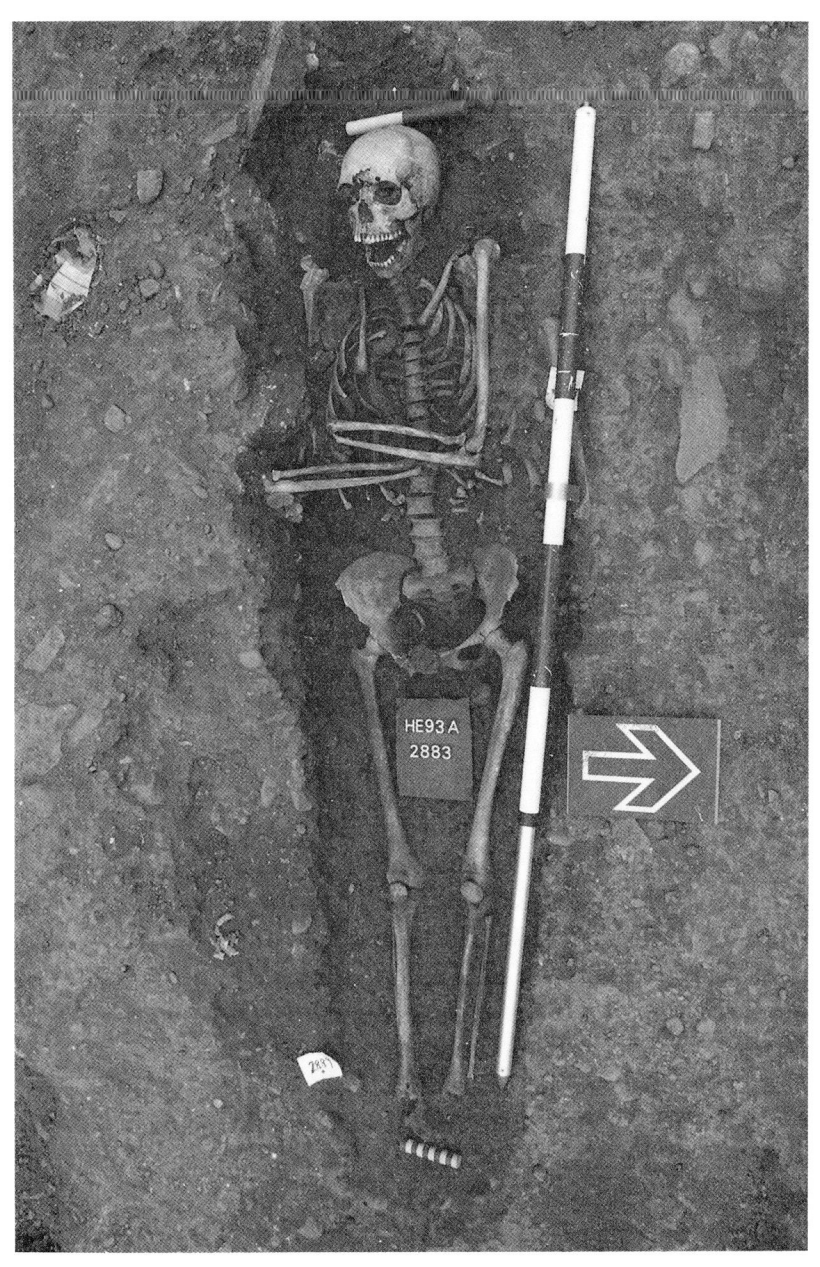

Fig. 35. Skeleton 2883, the arms folded across the stomach

also a number of differing alignments of the bodies, varying by as much as 30 degrees. These differences perhaps indicate the position or orientation of major buildings or paths in the area at the time of burial.

Alongside the changes in the way that the body was laid out, the receptacle for the body also changed with time. The stone lining of several of the early burials consisted of flat slabs of local stone laid against the side of the grave. They were rarely complete, in some cases because of intercutting by later graves, but in others the lining was concentrated solely around the upper body, particularly the head. This practice seems to have been quite short lived in Hereford, though in some parts of the country where stone was more plentiful it lasted from the Saxon period through to the seventeenth century, or even later.

In two graves evidence was found of a coffin where some of the wood survived with wooden joints or pegs, but no nails. This method may have been common, but survival of any evidence at all is rare. Once iron nails started to be used the presence of a coffin becomes easier to establish, though many of the nails were probably not in their primary positions due to the disintegration of the wood. However, all the indications are that the most common practice was to bury the dead without a coffin, a simple shroud being used. This practice appears to have been used throughout the life of the cemetery.

Social Status
It is notoriously hard to identify any differences in the social status of the dead, not least because it is not known in what form, if any, graves were marked. Certainly, from the degree of intercutting found in this part of the cathedral cemetery, the marking can only have been temporary. It is well known that citizens above a certain status, the Great and the Good, would have been buried within the cathedral itself, but a wide diversity of social classes would still have been interred in the cemetery.

Generally, there was a certain amount of segregation, particularly in later years, in the choice of a burial location, particularly with regard to the church. The south side was generally favoured whilst the north side might be reserved for excommunicates, suicides and others of dubious status (Gittings, 1984).

Because of the position of the cathedral and its associated buildings, much of the area south of the cathedral was not available for general burial. Those buried near the east end, close to the altar, were generally of higher status than those buried further to the west. This would suggest that those buried at this western limit of the cemetery should in general be of low status. Indeed, the use of this area for the mass graves in the middle of the fourteenth century would support this theory. However, the presence of apparently high status burials, such as 3616 with its mortar monument base, could argue against it.

One possibility is that for at least some of the lifetime of the cemetery this area was reserved for the deceased from the parish of St John. The road immediately to the west of the graveyard, now called Palace Yard, used to be known as St John's Place. The parish of St John was made up of parcels of land all over the city, including the central core, and had no church of its own, being served by an altar in the cathedral. If it is the case that the skeletons are all from this parish then they could well represent all the social classes.

The area in which there were twelve child burials to the south of the main area excavated may indicate that for some time there was a separate part of the graveyard devoted to children.

One possibility being investigated is that of recognising family links from genetic variations seen in the skeletons. Some had extra growth of bone on specific ribs, in others there was a failure to close the metopic suture in the skull, usually fused in adulthood, giving rise to what is known as the 'Inca' bone. Both these conditions are genetically controlled and with further study could enable family groups to be extracted from the assemblage.

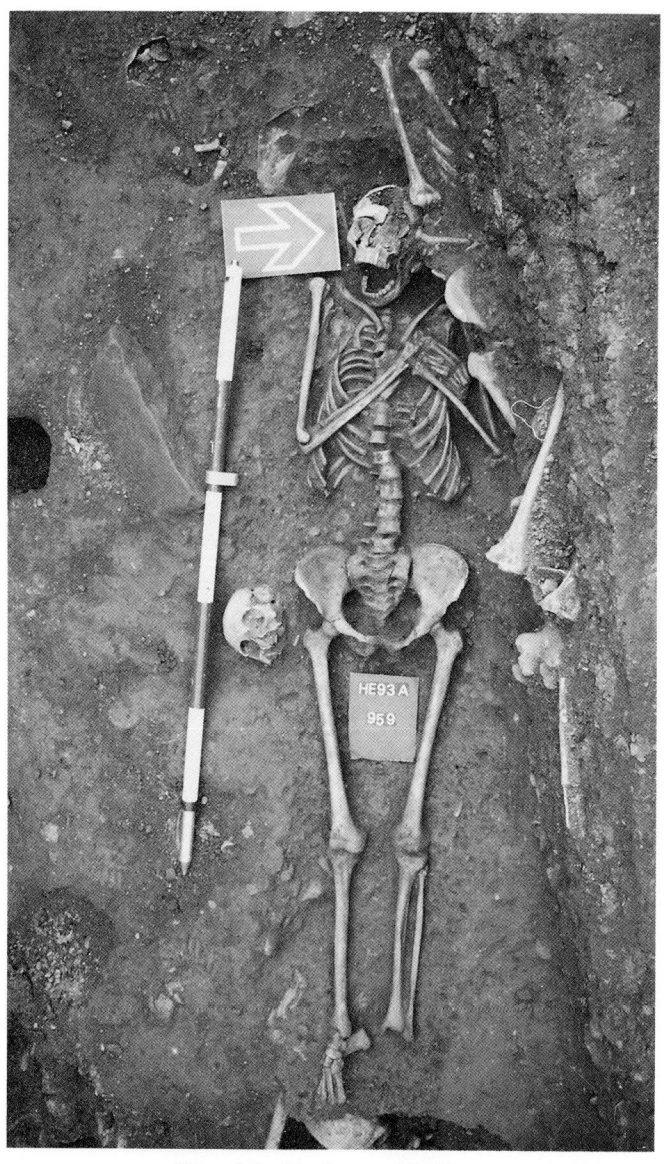

Fig. 36. Skeleton 0959, the arms folded on the chest

The whole area to the west of the cloister had apparently ceased to be used as a burial ground by the beginning of the seventeenth century.

THE POST-MEDIEVAL USE (Period 5) (Fig. 37)

Description

A deep oval pit (0079), 4.9 metres long and 2.5 metres wide, was excavated through the central mass grave of the medieval cemetery. It was dug into the natural gravels, to a total depth of almost two metres, and was backfilled with soil and angular sandstone fragments (Fig. 38). It was also rich in animal and plant remains.

Further east, beyond the mass graves, a small number of pits also cut through the cemetery levels. One of the pits (0077) was filled entirely with human bone, probably found when other pits were dug. Another

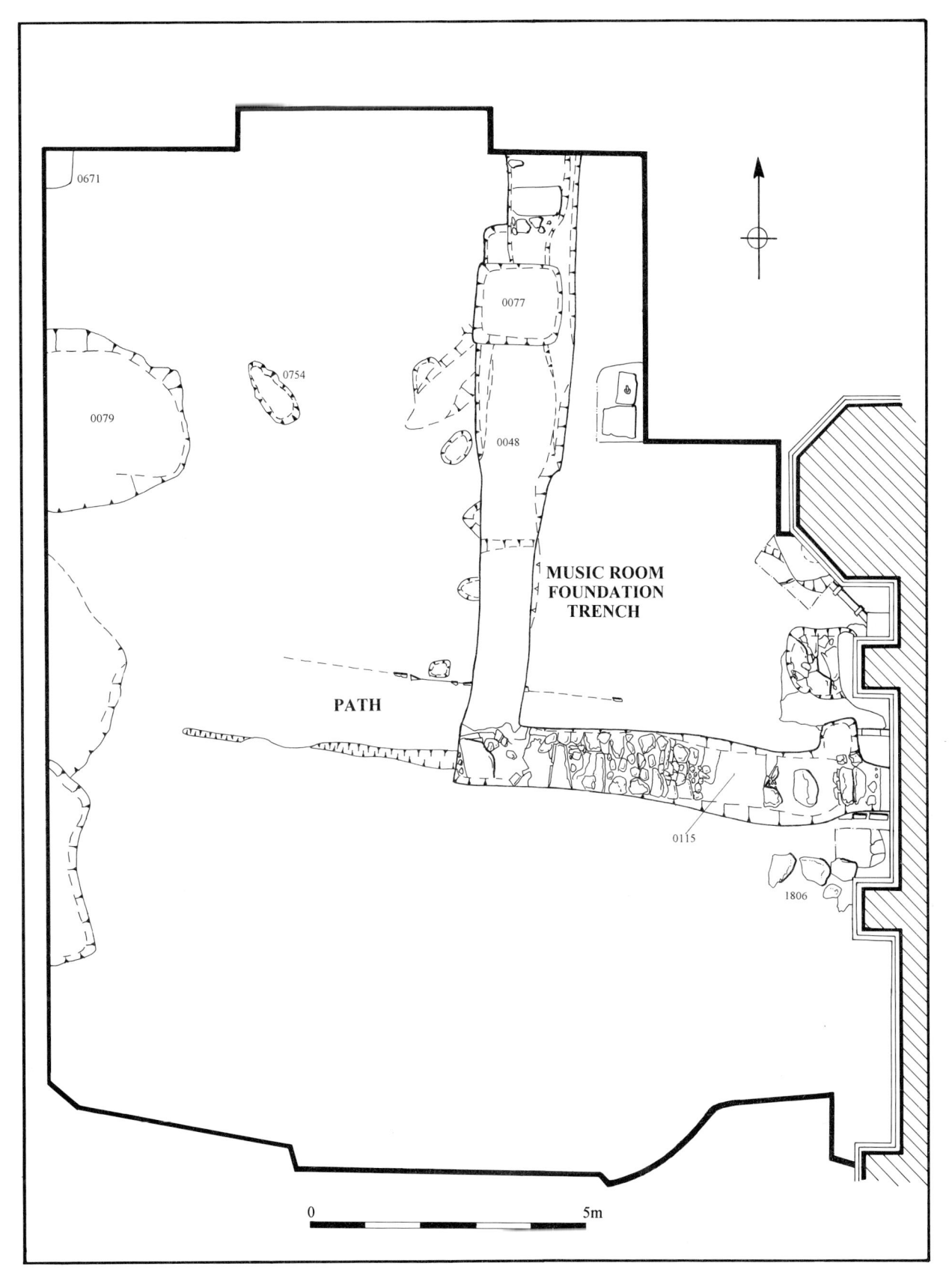

Fig. 37. Plan of the excavation, Period 5

pit (0754) which was filled with a humic soil, was very rich in environmental evidence and produced remains of textiles, a copper alloy belt fitting, and an almost complete pot. Further pits along the western side of the site also suggest the use of this area by some other household or minor industrial occupation. These features date from the seventeenth century onwards and relate to the use of the site as a garden, and later as a timber yard.

At the extreme north-west of the site was the corner of a wall (0671), built of tufa. This was a feature that had been detected on the radar survey and cut through the northern mass grave. Another short stretch of sandstone masonry (1806), with an east-west alignment, was present towards the south-east of the site.

In the eastern part of the site were parts of the south and west foundation trenches (0048) of the 1760 Music Room. The trenches were 1.2 metres wide and dug to varying depths. To the south the depth was 1.5 metres, but along the western trench, after a distance of some 4 metres, the depth was reduced to 1.2 metres. At the south the foundations of reused masonry bonded with a hard mortar had been left in situ (0115). Some of this stone consisted of elaborate architectural fragments, mainly of Perpendicular style.

Where the foundation stones had been robbed out of the trench, the backfill material was made up of demolition material from the Music Room coupled with other rubbish of the period. It consisted of brick rubble and other building debris, including slate, together with bottles, coins and clay pipes, probably belonging to the workmen on the site in 1835, the year when the building was demolished.

Many shallow features of this period must have been lost or severely truncated when the ground was lowered in 1851.

Fig. 38. Pit 0079

After that date disturbances to the ground were slight and consisted of pits for planting, paths and modern service trenches.

Discussion

The pit, 0079, may have been dug to extract gravel by the masons working on the cathedral or its ancillary buildings and the upper fill is probably derived from the masons' chippings. The pottery evidence indicates that it was probably dug in the sixteenth century when that area was beyond the currently accepted boundary of the cemetery. It must be assumed that the presence of the mass graves had been forgotten by that time. The only major work of that date associated with the cathedral was the construction of Bishop Booth's porch over the north door and it is possible that the chippings derive from that construction. A shallow seventeenth century rubbish pit produced much domestic pottery suggesting that this area was no longer considered to be a burial ground. Eighteenth century rubbish pits that cut across pit 0079 were probably associated with the timber yard or other buildings on the Palace Yard frontage. Taking all the evidence together it would appear that this part of the site ceased to be used as a cemetery some time during the sixteenth century.

The foundation trench, 0048, was that of the Music Room, built in 1762 to replace the west range of the cloister which had just been demolished. The Music Room was itself demolished in 1835. The finds from the backfill of the trench confirm the documentary and graphic evidence that the building was substantially of brick, plastered internally and roofed with slate. The majority of the stone recovered from the foundations clearly came from the demolished fifteenth century west range of the cloister, though some fragments of twelfth to fourteenth century masonry were also recovered. The south-western corner of the Music Room was directly over the charnel pit and it was in this area that the foundation trench was deepest. Even so, it was well above the bottom of the earlier pit and there would have been potential for settlement in this part of the building—perhaps another reason for its demolition.

The lowering of the ground surface in 1851 was widespread throughout the whole of the Close as is shown by early prints. In most areas, burials have been encountered from time to time just below the surface. From that time on the site has only been used as a public space and garden, with minimal damage from small pits for planting shrubs.

The Finds

The Artefacts *by Ros Tyrell*

The comments that follow are made before any conservation work has been carried out and without the benefit of any form of independent dating. They should be taken as a brief overview to be amended following a full study.

The finds provide an interesting and varied insight into life in Hereford from the late Saxon to the post-medieval period, for in addition to the burials a number of rubbish pits were dug into the site over the years.

However, the use of the site as a burial ground is the main feature and it is from the graves that many objects of interest were unearthed. Unfortunately, the density of the burials means that it was seldom possible to be sure that objects found in graves were intentionally deposited in them. Notable exceptions to this are the iron barrel padlocks found on the pelvic areas of 3843 (an adolescent) and 4215 (an adult female), both dating to the late Saxon period (Fig. 39). It is uncertain exactly what these objects represent, though judging by the textile impressions, presumably of the shroud, the locks were placed in the graves at burial rather than being some form of coffin fastening. There may be parallels elsewhere for such finds.

Some of the finds from features not associated with burials still have possible funerary connections and have been tentatively identified as such. Although there was no decorative copper alloy or white metal alloy coffin furniture, eight fragmentary iron coffin handles were recovered. Three copper alloy tacks, possibly for attaching texts or prayers to a coffin, were also found. The majority of the 3,382 iron nails are likely to be from coffins and many preserve fragments of the wood into which they had been nailed.

Amongst the finds there are seven copper alloy finger rings, a complex copper alloy wire

Fig. 39. Barrel padlock, Period 2

Fig. 40. Shroud buckle, with leather, Period 4

ornament with bone beads, five copper alloy hose hooks (or hooked tags), nine copper alloy dress pins, fifteen buttons (12 copper alloy, 2 bone & 1 glass), two bracelets, a brooch pin and six beads (3 glass, 2 bone & 1 chalk). All these are items of personal adornment that may have been worn by the occupants of the graves, in which case they would have funerary associations. However, they may equally have been dropped or deposited with rubbish. Of the twelve possible shroud buckles (copper alloy, white metal alloy & iron) only one was directly associated with a skeleton. Although the metal is badly corroded two fragments of the leather are preserved looped around the buckle frame (Fig. 40). The others were loose in graves or the surrounding soil.

Unusually for a non-water-logged site some scraps of textile were found. Those from non-burial features are very similar to those from an early grave and the fabric impressions on the padlocks. One scrap was found adhering to a copper alloy buckle and may be datable more closely than just to the medieval period.

The iron sword with a pattern-welded blade found in the cesspit in the late Saxon basement has been examined at both the Royal Armouries and the Ancient Monuments Laboratory of English Heritage. It has been provisionally dated to the eleventh century but could possibly be earlier (Brian Gilmour pers. comm.). The hilt was possibly horn whilst the scabbard was made from ash (Jacqui Watson pers. comm.) (Fig. 41).

A copper alloy harness fitting of early medieval date and a slightly later book clasp and strap (Fig. 42) were unfortunately both found in later features. Four spindle whorls came from the late Saxon/early Norman period. A piece of decorated worked bone may be a handle (Fig. 43).

The post-medieval finds are much more varied and include a complete glass inkwell and an apothecary's bottle, wig curlers and an unusual group of bone apple corers, including fragments associated with their manufacture (Fig. 44).

The glass finds consist mostly of pieces of seventeenth and eighteenth century wine bottles, but include fragments of at least one earlier jar with a frilled base. Several fragments of medieval painted window glass presumably came from the cathedral or the demolished cloistral range.

Crucible fragments found in the earliest levels indicate some industrial activity on the site. The only other evidence of industry is the manufacture of apple corers in the post-medieval period. However, crumbs, lumps, dribbles and scraps of iron, copper alloy and lead were recovered from all periods. A total of 29 flints were also recovered from all periods, including two scrapers and one other possible tool.

The fragments of clay pipes include several stamps, all of which appear to be of local manufacture.

Fig. 41. Sword, Period 2

Fig. 42. Book clasp

Fig. 43. Bone object, possibly a handle

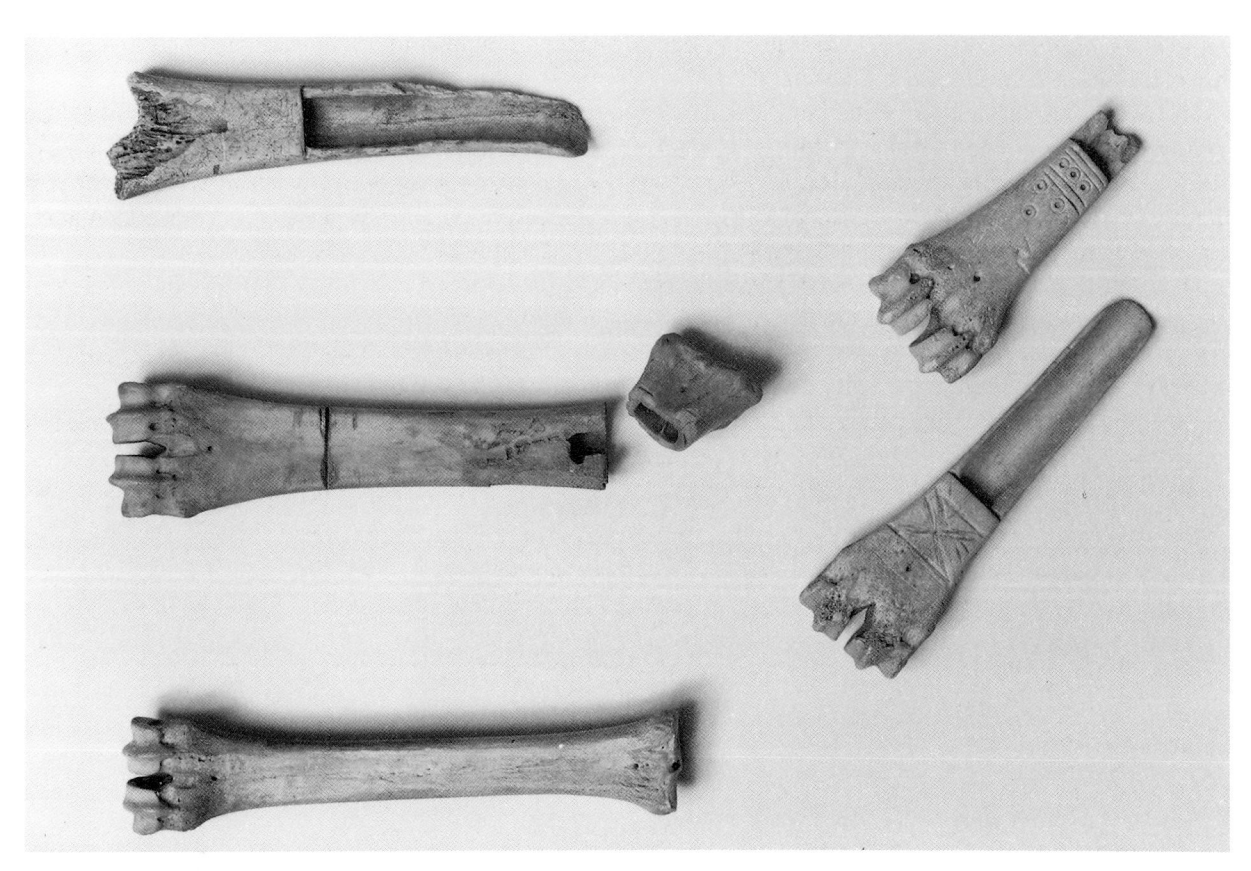

Fig. 44. Apple corers, Period 5

The Coins *by Nic Appleton-Fox*

28 coins were recovered from the excavation, together with a collection of copper alloy discs and wire from the late Saxon period, which may represent coins. These have not been cleaned or properly examined by a specialist, so the following is simply an outline description.

The earliest coin found was associated with a skeleton from the eleventh century cemetery. It is a cut quarter of a penny apparently of William I 'Paxs' type, datable to between 1066 and 1087. A coin from the fill of the gravel quarry is of copper alloy but is presently too encrusted to identify.

Three silver and two copper alloy coins were recovered from the medieval cemetery. The copper alloy examples will need cleaning before they can be identified, and they may be jettons or counters rather than coins. One of the silver coins, a cut half of a penny, is of Short Cross design (1180-1247). Another also has a cross, but the form is uncertain, though it may be an example of the new coinage of Edward I (1278-1307). The third has a Tudor shield design and is probably of sixteenth century date. Two silver coins from a post-medieval pit are probably of similar date, and two copper coins may also be early post-medieval. The rest of the coins are of copper alloy and are probably of nineteenth century date, 13 of the 19 coming from the backfill of the Music Room foundation trench.

The Human Remains *by Stephanie Pinter-Bellows*

Throughout the area excavated there was a total of 1,129 recognisable inhumations. Many were only partial skeletons as they had been disturbed by later burials. The disturbances had resulted in a considerable amount of disarticulated human bone found in most layers and graves. The loose bone was recorded in terms of quantity but is not included in this overall analysis. The disarticulated bone from the charnel pit was not examined during the excavation due to the exceptional quantity. It is estimated that there were in excess of 5,000 individuals represented.

All the skeletons were examined in the ground as the excavation progressed and this report is based on that examination. A record was made, where possible, of the age, sex, and proportion of the skeleton present and any obvious pathologies. Measurements were taken of long bones when it was thought that the skeleton could not be lifted intact. The nature of this examination has meant that the information collected was variable and the data should only be treated as a guide to the skeletons.

The preservation of the skeletal material ranged from good to very poor, most of the bones being in fair condition. The completeness of the skeletons has been affected, not only by the degree of preservation, but also by the intercutting of the graves. Thus only 13% of the skeletons (150) were complete and undisturbed whilst in 24% of the cases (262) less than a quarter had survived *in situ*.

The sex of adolescent and adult skeletons can be determined using standard measuring criteria, providing suitable bones survive. An assessment can also be made of age. The preliminary analysis is shown in the table below. While a full range of adolescent and adult skeletons, male and female, have been represented in the sample excavated, juveniles, and in particular infants, are under-represented[1].

	Males	Females	Sex not determined	Totals
Foetal/Newborn	-	-	5	5
Up to 2 years	-	-	17	17
2-5 years	-	-	27	27
5-10 years	-	-	49	49
10-15 years	-	-	29	29
15-20 years	8	4	12	24
Young adults (about 20-30 years)	24	36	4	64
Middle aged (about 30-50 years)	41	43	6	90
Old (over 50 years)	10	15	6	31
'Under 15'*	-	-	106	106
'Adults'*	116	125	168	409
Uncertain age or unexamined*	-	-	278	278
Totals	199	223	707	1,129

Table showing preliminary analysis of ages of skeletons at death
* The high number of skeletons where details of age and sex have not been determined is due to the preliminary nature of the examination, and the varying degree of disturbance

1. The methods used are presented in Bass (1971), Stewart (1979) and the Workshop of European Anthropologists (1980). Priority for gender determination was given to pelvis shape where differences are associated with reproduction. Skull shape, measurements of the femur and humerus head, and the glenoid fossa of the scapula, and other robusticity characteristics were evaluated for differences in size and muscularity. Sexing of children's skeletons is controversial and difficult and was not attempted.

Sub-adult age was determined through dental development (Logan and Kronfeld as presented in Downer, 1975) and bone fusion (Krogman, 1962; Brothwell, 1972). Adult age was evaluated using the recommendations of the Workshop of European Anthropologists (1980) and changes to the auricular surface of the pelvis by Lovejoy et al. (1985). The regularity of adult bone ageing processes is under debate, as is the precision and accuracy to which adult skeletal age can be estimated. The adults, therefore, were roughly divided into three groups when it was possible to age them in the ground: Young adults (20-30), Middle-aged adults (30-50), and Old adults (50+). As children's development is considered to be a more regular process than that of adults, they have been divided into more age categories: Foetal - Newborn, Newborn - 2 years, 2-5, 5-10, 10-15, 15-20.

The pathologies noted below are a sample of what will be ascertained with full analysis, as only those obvious during the excavation and the lifting of still-uncleaned skeletons are described. Criteria for probable diagnosis stem from Steinbock (1976) and Ortner and Putschar (1981). Pathologies have been divided into congenital and acquired diseases.

Congenital diseases observed range from minor anomalies which may never have been noticed by the individual affected through to fatal abnormalities. Several minor anomalies of skeletal development were found that would have affected the vertebral column and ribs. There is a sizable minority of specimens with transitional vertebrae (those where the shape of the vertebra partially resembles that of a neighbouring type). This has occurred particularly with the fifth lumbar and the first sacral vertebrae. Fusion of the fifth and sixth ribs and of various neighbouring cervical and upper thoracic vertebrae was also observed. Retention of the metopic suture, the place of union of the two halves of the frontal bone on the skull which usually disappears in early childhood, was recorded. While the variation in influence of genetic as against environmental factors such as general living conditions has not been studied for the congenital characteristics, these anomalies may well be useful in establishing genetic relationships within a population.

Two instances in which a congenital abnormality would have presented significant symptoms to the individual concerned have been noted. One is a possible case of hydrocephalus: this occurs when fluid does not drain correctly from around the brain causing pressure and eventually an enlargement of the skull. This affects the functioning of the brain, leaving the individual dependent on those around them for care. The second case was an adolescent with a case of scoliosis of the spine. This curvature of the spine would have affected movement and was probably one of several problems that this individual suffered, leading to an early death.

The majority of the acquired diseases have been identified as arthropathies and degenerative diseases. Osteoarthrosis, or degenerative joint disease, especially of the vertebral column, was observed in many of the adults, becoming especially obvious in middle age. It is an ubiquitous accompaniment of advancing age and can also be a secondary phenomenon following other pathological processes such as fractures. Changes include additional bone formation at the margins of the joints; destruction of cartilage at the joint, in some cases leading to bone rubbing against bone; localised destruction of bone in the joint; and sometimes fusion of joints.

Another arthropathy which was noted are several cases of DISH (diffuse idiopathic skeletal hyperostosis). This is chiefly manifested by calcification of ligaments which, as ligaments are located near particular joint surfaces, limits movement. It also occurs as extra bone growth on the side of the front part of the vertebrae, sometimes leading to fusion and thus possibly affecting movement. Its cause is unknown, but there are some associations with adult diabetes, obesity, gout and chronic excessive levels of vitamin A.

Trauma was seen mostly as healed fractures of limbs. The majority of these fractures were without large swellings at the site of the break but with some over-ride of the fragmented ends. There were also at least two cases of pseudarthosis of fractures in the lower arm. This occurs when the fragmented ends do not knit, but instead continue to have a certain amount of movement leading to an artificial joint. There was one unhealed fracture of the fibula, tentatively diagnosed by the position of fragmented bone found during the excavation. Two examples of skull fractures were identified, one of which is believed to have proved fatal. A healed blade wound was also observed.

Infectious diseases are mostly represented in non-specific forms, where the bacteria or virus which caused them are not known. It mainly affected the fibrous covering of the bone (the periosteum, the infection to the bone termed periostitis), especially localised to the lower leg. This is often caused by repeated injury to the shins or from ulcers resulting from varicose veins. A more general covering of periostitis was observed on the bones of two of the infant skeletons. This could perhaps be part of weanling syndrome, when, due to weaning on to less than optimal foods, a cycle of malnutrition and infections leads to death. Specific infectious disease was seen in several cases of tuberculosis, noted as lesions on the vertebrae.

The dental health of the population as a whole appears to be quite good with few cavities or lost teeth obvious; though abscesses—localised areas of infection—are in evidence. The low frequency of cavities implies that the diet was not high in the sugars and starches that cause such decay. Several cases of enamel hypoplasia were noted. This consists of an area with a deficiency of enamel which occurs during the development of the tooth. It occurs during severe stress and has been associated with general disorders and nutritional deficiency.

A few cases of metabolic disease have been found. Metabolic diseases are a loose category consisting of dietary and hormonal abnormalities of deficiency or excess; they can be caused by chronic or acute problems. One infant skull was observed with porotic hyperostosis; this thickening of the bones of the skull is usually a response to chronic anaemia, often caused by iron deficiency. There were also several cases of cribra orbitalia, where there is a thickening in the bone of the roof of the eye. Its cause is not completely understood—it is often thought to be associated with chronic anaemia, but may be caused by a localised infection or scurvy. The skull of one infant showed a suspected case of scurvy, which is caused by a vitamin C deficiency. There were also several cases of spina bifida occulta, which is a failure of the bony spinal canal of the vertebrae to completely form; this mild type of spina bifida would not be noticed by the individual. It is thought to be caused by a lack of folic acid, part of the B vitamin complex, though there may also be a genetic component in that in some families the foetus may be more likely not to form the complete canal when there is a lack of folic acid.

The only neoplastic disease, or tumour, so far diagnosed has been several benign bony osteomas. They are harmless and usually symptomless, semicircular bony projections, which occur when some cells in the upper-most layer of bone grow more than surrounding tissue for a short while. They can vary in size but are usually about that of a pea.

The Animal Bone *by Stephanie Pinter-Bellows*

17,096 animals bones with a total weight of 133.4 kg were recovered from the excavation. The largest amount (37% by weight) was from the late Saxon occupation (Period 2). The animal bones were counted, weighed and a note was made of the number of species present as the excavation progressed. The more obvious signs of any burning, gnawing or butchery, whether the edges of the fragments were sharp or dull, their colour, and any pathologies were also noticed.

As is normal in most urban excavations, the bones of cattle, sheep and/or goat (not easy to differentiate) and pig were common. The various domestic species of bird ranked next, with those of chickens being more numerous than those of geese. The next most common bone was that of horse, whilst both deer bone and antler were recovered. Several dog and cat burials were found. Amongst the minor species represented on the site were rabbit, duck, pigeon, crow and frog or toad. There was the occasional bone from rodent and fish, but they have not yet been assigned to species.

A post-medieval pit, from which two sixteenth century coins were found, also contained bones of rabbit, roe deer, chicken, goose, and fish, perhaps from a high status table. The late Saxon (Period 2) pits include a mixture of bones that are far less food oriented, such as a cow's skull, roe deer, goat horncores, and a minimum of two dogs and two cats.

There were very few cases where signs of gnawing and swallowing were noted. Most of the gnawing was probably carried out by dogs. The bones which show the characteristic erosion of stomach acid were probably swallowed by dogs, though pigs cannot be ruled out. Gnawing is more likely to have taken place when bones were left on the surface for some length of time instead of being quickly buried.

A larger proportion than normal of the bones in the late Saxon period had signs of burning. Only a small percentage of the bones examined had obvious butchery marks. As anticipated, these were found mainly on cow bones where the size of the animal leads to more divisions of the carcass.

Pathologies seen on a small percentage of bones included periostitis, a non-specific infection of the outer layer of the bone. There were also examples of eburnation, where bone rubbed against bone in a joint because the cartilage had been destroyed; spavin, exostoses of the tarsus, in this case causing ankylosis of the tarsus and metatarsus; and a healed fracture.

The Ceramic Material *by Alan Vince*

The ceramic material from the excavation consisted of 2,780 sherds of pottery, 340 pieces of tile and 340 brick fragments. The preliminary examination has concentrated on material from the earlier periods and specifically on information that is of help in dating the various occupation levels.

Pottery is described by means of differing fabrics (utilising differences in the rock and minerals in the object's clay) according to a system first published for Hereford in 1985. (Vince, 1985 a). Under this system, fabrics are coded by letters and numbers. The initial letter gives an indication of the source of the pottery: A for Herefordshire, B for The Malverns, C for Worcestershire, D for The Cotswolds, E is non-local, F for French, and G is of unknown origin. The remainder of the code refers to a specific fabric, with numbers indicating style and usage. These codes are shown in brackets where appropriate.

The earliest settlement (Period 1)

The eleven fragments of tile found in features of this period are all definitely of Romano-British date. There were only five potsherds and all are of types that could occur in period 2, including one from the Malverns (fabric B1) that was first produced in the late eleventh century. These few sherds of pottery may be intrusive and do not provide any information whatsoever about the occupation of the site.

The late Saxon period (Period 2)

The various features in this period contained much pottery, including some residual Romano-British material. The pottery includes sherds which have previously been recognised as occurring in Hereford in the later tenth to eleventh centuries (G1) and in the later eleventh and twelfth centuries (D2). It is significant that there are no sherds of the early tenth to early eleventh century Cotswold ware (D1) from this period, indeed there is only one such sherd from the entire excavation. In Hereford this ware has consistently been found in association with fabric G1 particularly in the late tenth and early eleventh century. There is a similar absence of late ninth and early tenth century Stamford ware also found elsewhere in Hereford in association with G1 cooking pots.

In Gloucester, fabric D2 cooking pots have been shown to have progressed from everted rimmed globular vessels to club-rimmed cylindrical vessels and globular vessels with flat-topped everted rims. (Vince, 1985 b) Examples of all three types were found in this period, but the first type was the most common. Sherds of other unglazed cooking wares were also found but form a small proportion of the assemblage.

Glazed wares consist of pitchers probably of local manufacture (A7a), Stamford ware, Winchester-type ware and Minety ware (D3). The latter sherd is from a vessel with rectangular toothed roller-stamped decoration, the earliest type produced by that particular industry. At least three of the Stamford ware sherds are from vessels with a glossy yellow glaze, of a type which is characteristic of the early to mid eleventh century. There were also examples of a thin-glazed, late eleventh to mid twelfth century variety of Stamford ware. A small assemblage associated with this phase included a large fragment of a Stamford ware pitcher, of late eleventh to mid twelfth century date, as well as sherds of fabric D2. Of the six rim sherds of fabric D2, five were everted and one flat-topped everted.

Whilst pottery of both early to mid eleventh century and later eleventh to early twelfth century date is present in this period, it is not yet possible to say whether the G1 cooking pots and Stamford ware pitchers were deposited as fresh rubbish in the early eleventh century or were dumped on the site at a later date.

The charnel pit (Period 3)

The assemblage from this period is slightly larger than that from period 2 but is very similar in character, although the proportion of G1 cooking pots is lower and that of B1 cooking pots is higher, whilst D2 vessels are again by far the most common. A possible example of a Forest of Dean product (A8) was found. At Gloucester these vessels were thought to be of twelfth century date but at Monnow Street in Monmouth they occurred in the earliest phases of occupation, which were coin-dated to the late eleventh century. (*pers. comm.* S. Clarke, Monmouth Archaeological Society.)

All three of the rim types of fabric D2 occur in similar proportions to those found in period 2. Only 11 glazed sherds were found in total, a lower proportion than in the earlier period, and there are no sherds of tripod pitchers, all come from wheelthrown pitchers. The Stamford ware sherds include glossy-glazed examples which are probably residual.

The unglazed wares date the period to the very late eleventh century or later, whilst the absence of glazed tripod pitchers suggests a date not far into the twelfth century.

The medieval cemetery (Period 4)
The pottery from this period consists mainly of small scraps, some of which are too small to identify. A substantial quantity is of identical type to those found in periods 2 and 3. Once again no examples of B2 tripod pitchers were found whilst only 3 Worcestershire cooking pots (C1) occur in contrast to 146 D2 sherds (20 rim sherds, 18 everted and 2 clubbed). There is therefore a gap in pottery deposition between the end of period 3 (c.1100) and the beginning of this period. A few sherds of later twelfth to early thirteenth century wares were found which show that there is pottery in this assemblage made before c.1250, but over half of the pottery comes from fabric A7b glazed jugs and other late thirteenth to mid fourteenth century wares. Late medieval wares, dating to the later fourteenth and fifteenth centuries, were also present but not common. Two sherds of oxidised glazed Malvern (B4) conical cooking pots and at least some of the 36 sherds of B4 jug are probably of later fourteenth or fifteenth century date. However, the majority of the B4 sherds are from distinctive sixteenth century forms, such as pipkins, jars, lids and chafing dishes. An end date for this period in the early sixteenth century is indicated by the presence of sherds of dark-glazed cups in both sand-tempered (Cistercian ware) and fine local (A7c) fabrics. The low quantity of the Malvern fabric B5 and Hereford A7d vessels further suggests that the end date is before the end of the sixteenth century.

The post-medieval period (Period 5)
The pottery assemblage from one pit includes a high proportion of residual material, from Romano-British tile fragments through to the later medieval wares which characterise the latest elements of the period 4 assemblage. It also includes several smashed or semi-complete vessels. Taking only these vessels into account, a date in the sixteenth century, probably the early to middle years, seems likely. Imports are represented by sherds of South Netherlands tin-glazed ware and a Spanish mercury jar but not by Rhenish stonewares. The assemblage is dominated by vessels for food preparation rather than serving, as is particularly shown in the quantity of pipkins found.

Aside from this pit group only 22 sherds were examined from this period. They are a mixture of 4 sherds of residual eleventh and twelfth century material, 16 sherds of sixteenth century date of very similar character to those from the pit group and 3 sherds of nineteenth century or later wares. The only sixteenth century type found which is not present in the previous assemblage is a sherd of a Spanish red micaceous jar.

Local and Regional Importance
This site has produced an assemblage of eleventh to twelfth century pottery which is more than ten times larger than the next largest collection from Hereford. (Bewell Street, HE81E. Thomas, forthcoming). Regionally, the later eleventh and early twelfth centuries have attracted attention for two reasons: one as a result of discussions concerning the date and significance of the changeover in the West Midlands from wheelthrown Stafford ware and the like (G1 and D1) to handmade coarsewares such as fabric D2; the second due to the association of fabric D2 with early Anglo-Norman penetration into Wales (Clarke,1991) and, through trade, with Dublin (Vince, 1988). In both cases it would be extremely useful to be able to establish more securely the date and sequence of late eleventh and early twelfth century types.

The other material of interest is the sixteenth century pit group from period 5. Although material of this date is common in Hereford and more widely in the Welsh Marches and Severn Valley, there are different forms found in this collection, such as a standing costrel in Cistercian ware. Furthermore, the assemblage is clearly different in character from others found in Hereford which are dominated by the presence of jars and conical bowls and which contain imported stoneware.

The Environmental Remains *by Elizabeth Pearson*

Throughout the excavation an extensive programme of sampling for environmental remains was carried out in order to provide information on aspects of life such as diet, living conditions and industrial or agricultural economy. Many features were sampled including graves, hearths, burnt layers, pits, occupation surfaces and possible cesspit material. A large number of samples taken from graves has yet to be assessed. However, of the remaining 360 samples, a total of 29 from a variety of features of mostly eleventh or twelfth century date were selected for a preliminary assessment.

The samples were processed on-site by flotation and the plant remains were then examined using a microscope. Rich charred cereal remains were recovered from deposits directly below the late Saxon road surface. They were dominated by barley and appear to have been virtually clean of chaff and weed seeds, suggesting that they represent fully processed grain rather than the waste from crop cleaning. They were probably charred accidentally when the grain was dried prior to storage or milling. Drying would discourage spoilage resulting from fungal growth and parching would make milling easier. This may represent clean or semi-clean grain (requiring little further crop processing) being brought into the city from the surrounding countryside. Nevertheless, it must be borne in mind that the chaff of free-threshing crops like barley is easily destroyed by fire and may leave little trace in the archaeological record.

It is interesting that barley was the main grain found in this excavation, as other cereal crops found in Hereford have been generally mixed, with the exception of a few concentrated deposits of oats and rye of medieval date. Barley may have been ground to make flour and, although it was not particularly favoured for bread making, it was frequently used in gruel or soup. Although it was also the main cereal used for brewing beer, there was no evidence of malting to suggest its use for this purpose.

Deposits containing large quantities of mammal and fish bone, insect pupae, mineralized seeds and concretions were present in the cesspit fill of the late Saxon basement, and in a post-medieval pit from the southern part of the site. Cesspit deposits characteristically contain abundant phosphate concretions, fish bones and mineralized seeds, particularly those which are small enough to have been swallowed and passed through the human gut. Although there was evidence to indicate that larger items, such as fruit stones, animal bones and fish bones, were commonly swallowed, the bulk of the large quantities of mammal and fish bone and fruit stones in the pits must have come from domestic refuse. Mineralized material is generally assumed to have been caused by the presence of calcium phosphate from faeces. However, calcium phosphate also comes from bones and this may produce the same effect. It is therefore possible that the mineralized seeds and concretions found may have been partly a result of deposition with large quantities of fish bones. In effect, the mineralized remains are most likely to result from the mixing of a primary cesspit deposit with a later backfill of domestic rubbish.

A late Saxon hearth was of interest as it contained abundant burnt fish bone and occasional cremated mammal bone and bread wheat grains. They had obviously been burnt at a high temperature, and may represent the disposal of household rubbish within the hearth. Similar remains were found scattered over the site, possibly indicating a widespread method of waste disposal. However, such burning could possibly be coupled with fertiliser production to improve soils used for cultivation.

The fish and shellfish remains (not yet identified to species) indicate that this was an important source of food. Indeed, the abundance of fish bones from this site was remarkably high. Freshwater fish were probably caught locally in the river. Although recovered from features not necessarily connected with the cathedral, these remains may be an early reflection of the 'fish on Friday' custom. During the medieval period people were influenced by the dietary restrictions dictated by the church, which discouraged the consumption of meat and animal products on certain days. Fish was an acceptable alternative to 'meat' and allowed a degree of variability in the diet.

The range of fruits found was narrow and most could be collected locally. Elderberries and blackberries are likely to have been collected wild; and sloes, although sometimes cultivated in the past, would also have been readily available growing wild. Apple and pear trees were probably cultivated in orchards, and whilst figs can be grown in Britain under sheltered conditions they are most likely to have been imported.

The Future: what remains to be done

When the various official bodies concerned approved the plans to construct a new building for the Mappa Mundi and the Chained Library in Hereford Cathedral Close they insisted that the site should be archaeologically excavated, the remains properly recorded, and the results published in an appropriate form. The excavation has been completed—at a much greater cost than was originally anticipated, due to the unexpected depth of the charnel pit and the very large number of skeletons—but much work remains.

This is not a full publication—there is much analysis still to be done. During the excavation all the 1,129 skeletons retrieved, apart from the charnel material, were carefully washed, dried and packed away in bags and boxes ready for further study. This present report includes only the more obvious information, gathered whilst the skeletons were still in the ground and partly obscured by soil. The bones from the 5,000 or more people found in the charnel pit will not be examined—it has been decided that the academic return from a study of this disarticulated collection of bones would not warrant the cost involved. They have been reburied in consecrated ground.

Even so, the remaining skeletons comprise one of the largest collections of human remains that has been scientifically excavated in this country. Included amongst it are some examples from the late Saxon period, but the majority of the burials are medieval. A careful study of the intercutting relationships that have been established between the various burials will provide the information from which a 'generation' picture can be built up. Each skeleton will then be carefully examined by experts to establish the age, sex, height and any pathological information that may be available. Attempts will also be made to establish family relationships. The burials from the mass graves are of special interest for they provide a cross-section of the population over a very short period of time. At present all these remains are in store until sufficient additional funds have been obtained to carry out this massive piece of research.

This is not all, for during the excavation over 17,000 animal bones were found. They were rapidly assessed whilst the excavation was in progress and now await a full examination. The pottery and tile from the site has had a preliminary examination to provide information for dating the various occupation periods. Further examination of the more interesting groups will be needed and new types and varieties will have to be drawn for publication.

Soil samples were taken from many deposits on the site. These samples will provide the environmental information which will provide information on aspects of past life such as diet, living conditions and industrial or agricultural economy, in this important area of the city. So far only 29 of 360 samples have been examined. In addition a large number of samples were associated with graves and have yet to be assessed.

Small finds including brooches, buckles, padlocks, coins, fragments of material etc. have to be cleaned, possibly X-rayed, examined by specialists, and eventually photographed and drawn for the final publication.

Even when the problems of funding have been resolved, this project will take several years to complete. The final publication will provide a detailed assessment of a significant proportion of the population of this part of the country of several centuries. The features found during the excavation—the late Saxon road, the building with a basement, the vast pit and its grisly contents—are of immense importance in understanding the early history of Hereford and will be discussed and debated by archaeologists for many years to come.

Ron Shoesmith
Archaeological Consultant to the Dean and Chapter
and Director of the City of Hereford Archaeology Unit

Bibliography

Barrow, J, *Urban cemetery location in the high Middle Ages*, 78-100, in Bassett S, 1992
Barrow, J, (ed.), *English Episcopal Acta VII: Hereford 1079-1234*, 1993
Bass, W, *Human Osteology: A Laboratory and Field Manual of the Human Skeleton* Special Publications, 1971
Bassett, S, *Death in Towns*, 1992
Blair, J, The 12th-Century Bishop's Palace at Hereford *Medieval Archaeology* XXXI, 1987
Brothwell, D, *Digging Up Bones* Second Edition, 1972
Capes, W W, *Charters and Records of Hereford Cathedral*, 1908
Cart. Sax. W de G Birch, *Cartularium Saxonicum*, 3 vols. 1885-93
Clarke, S, *The Origins of Medieval Pottery* South-East Wales Medieval Ceram, 15, 29-36, 1991
Downer, G C, *Dental Morphology*, 1975
Duncumb, J. *History & Antiquities of the County of Hereford*, Volume I, 1804
Gittings, C, Death, *Burial and the Individual in Early Modern England*, 1984
Hamilton, N E S (ed.), *William of Malmesbury, Gesta Pontificum*, Rolls Series, 1870
Hughes, P, Report on Initial Documentary Research on the Excavation in Hereford Cathedral Close, (unpublished typescript), 1994
Humfrys, W S, *Memories of Old Hereford*, 1925
Krogman, W, *The Human Skeleton in Forensic Medicine*, 1962
Lovejoy, C O, Meindl, R, Mensforth, R, and Barton T, 'Chronological Metamorphosis of the Auricular surface of the Ilium: A New Method for the Determination of Adult Skeletal Age at Death', *American Journal of Physical Anthropology*, 68:1 5-28, 1985
Marshall, G, 'The Defences of the City of Hereford', *Trans. Woolhope Natur. Fld. Club*, XXX, 67-78, 1940
Morgan, P E, 'The Cathedral Close', *Friends of Hereford Cathedral*, Fifty-first Annual Report, 1976
Morris, J, (ed.), *Domesday Book: Herefordshire*, 1983
Ortner, D and Putschar, W 'Identification of Pathological Conditions in Human Skeletal Remains', *Smithsonian Contributions to Anthropology*, 28, 1981
Richards, J, *Viking Age England*, 1991
Shoesmith, R, *Hereford City Excavations 1, Excavations at Castle Green*, CBA Res. Rep. 36, 1980
Shoesmith, R, *Hereford City Excavations 2, Excavations on and close to the defences*, CBA Res. Rep. 46, 1982
Shoesmith, R, *Hereford City Excavations 3, The Finds*, CBA Res. Rep. 56, 1985
Shoesmith, R, *Hereford, History & Guide*, 1992
Steinbock, R T, *Paleopathological Diagnosis and Interpretation: Bone Disease in Ancient Human Populations*, 1976
Stewart, T D, *Essentials of Forensic Anthropology*, 1979
Thomas, A. *Excavations in Hereford 1976-90*, forthcoming
Vince, A G, 'The Ceramic Finds' in Shoesmith, 1985
Vince, A G, 'The Late Saxon, Medieval and Post-Medieval Pottery', in Saville, A (ed.) 'Salvage recording of Romano-British, Saxon, Medieval and Post-Medieval remains at North Street, Winchcombe, Gloucestershire', *Trans. Bristol Gloucestershire Archaeol. Soc.* 103, 113-23, 1985 b

Vince, A G, 'English Medieval Pottery in Viking Dublin' in Mac Niocall, Gearoid & Wallace. Patrick F (eds.) *Keimelia: Studies in Medieval Archaeology and History in Memory of Tom Delaney*, 254-70, Galway University Press, 1988

Watkins, A, 'The King's Ditch of the City of Hereford', *Trans. Woolhope Natur. Fld. Club*, XXIII, 249-58, 1920

White, W J, *The Cemetery of St Nicholas Shambles*, 1988

Whitehead, D, 'Historical introduction' in Shoesmith, 1980

Willis, R, 'Report of a survey of the delapidated portions of Hereford Cathedral in the year 1841' in *Architectural History of some English Cathedrals - Part II*, 1973

Workshop of European Anthropologists 'Recommendation for age and sex determination', *Journal of Human Evolution* 9:51 7-549, 1980